A. PETERS

The Iron Legion

Copyright © 2024 by A. Peters

All rights reserved. No part of this publication may be reproduced, stored or transmitted in any form or by any means, electronic, mechanical, photocopying, recording, scanning, or otherwise without written permission from the publisher. It is illegal to copy this book, post it to a website, or distribute it by any other means without permission.

This novel is entirely a work of fiction. The names, characters and incidents portrayed in it are the work of the author's imagination. Any resemblance to actual persons, living or dead, events or localities is entirely coincidental.

First edition

Contents

1 Chapter 1: Into the Forest   1
2 Chapter 2: Signs of the Enemy   23
3 Chapter 3: The Scattered Intelligence   43
4 Chapter 4: Retrieving the Truth   70
5 Chapter 5: The Return Path   99
6 Chapter 6: The Price of Duty   123

1

Chapter 1: Into the Forest

Scene 1.1: Emperor's Orders

The sun was already beginning its descent as the afternoon wore on. The ancient forest of Germania, a realm of gnarled oaks and whispering pines, swallowed the sun's rays, casting long, dancing shadows across the forest floor. The canopy of leaves intertwined, permitting only slivers of sunlight to pierce the emerald depths. The dirt trail, barely visible beneath a carpet of decaying leaves, twisted and turned through the dense undergrowth, disappearing at times under knotted roots and scattered rocks. The only sounds were the whisper of leaves underfoot and the soft clink of armor as Falco's century advanced. Their mission, their solemn obligation to their fellow soldiers, was clear: find the missing scouts or any trace of their intelligence, a duty they were bound to uphold, no matter the cost. Those scouts, sent ahead to track the stirrings of a Germanic uprising, had vanished without a trace.

Centurion Falco led his men with practiced caution, his senses hyperalert. His gaze darted from shadow to shadow, always searching, always anticipating. His left hand was firm on his shield, his right ready to draw his gladius. Behind him, his men moved silently, their fingers brushing their weapons. One signal—a raised fist—stopped them all. The century froze, breaths held. One nod—that's all it took for Varro. Falco's optio had an uncanny way of catching his signals, almost as if he could hear the unspoken commands. Years of fighting shoulder to shoulder had fused their instincts. Without a word, Varro melted back down the line, passing the command in silent, subtle gestures.

The soldiers shifted, shields snugged in a bit closer, hands gripping hilts like lifelines. Then, with a slow breath, they began moving again, and the silence—strange, almost heavy—settled around them. It wasn't just any quiet; it was the kind that grew from unspoken things, from a trust in their centurion that didn't need words.

"Shields in place. For Rome and honor—hold to your pairs," Falco's voice was barely a breath, yet it cut through the tension. He knew the men were nervous, especially young Titus, whose eyes darted around like a cornered hare.

"Titus, eyes to the treeline." Titus, startled by the quiet reprimand, straightened and adjusted his shield. "Right," he mumbled, his cheeks flushing.

A few of the men exchanged quick glances. They had trained for this, day after day, until each movement was as familiar as breathing. But training was one thing; facing the reality of those shadowed woods was another. Falco had seen lines collapse before, a gap appearing, and men left alone, vulnerable, their shields no longer overlapping. Chaos would surge in.

CHAPTER 1: INTO THE FOREST

The forest of Germania was different. The air crackled with a palpable sense of foreboding. Falco's thoughts drifted back to other forests, other hunts. Shadowed places where silence pressed in, thick and heavy. This cursed forest felt the same—the air itself a malevolent force. Always a warning if you knew how to hear it, he reminded himself. But what if he'd missed it? Ahead of him, the century stood like a spear in the gloom. They were the shield against the chaos threatening the Emperor's advance. And if the shield cracked here, in these woods, it wasn't just their lives at stake. It was the whole campaign unraveling. Germania wasn't just some nameless forest—it was the heart of the northern frontier.

He clenched his fists, jaw tight. The missing advance scouts had hinted at something larger, something coordinated—Germanic tribes pulling together, building a storm strong enough to uproot Rome itself. If the coalition wasn't broken here, the Emperor's grip on the frontier would be lost. Leading men into danger wasn't new to him. But this time, the stakes were different. This was politics, power, the kind of failure that echoed in the corridors of Rome.

He turned, eyes catching on the shadowed figures behind him. Faces partially hidden in the gloom, but their eyes—clear enough—fixed on him. Trusting him. He felt the weight of that trust, heavier than any shield. He couldn't break it. The forest held its breath, and so did he.

A primal instinct, honed from countless battles, told him to trust his gut. They were approaching the spot where the advance scouts had vanished. Their disappearance was a stark reminder of the hidden dangers.

The century continued their journey towards the last known location of the advance scouts, having covered four miles in the first four hours, but with many more still lying ahead. The approach of Tribune Severus broke the quiet. Severus, his crimson-trimmed tunic too bright for this place, rode up with impatience in his eyes. Young, full of ambition, Severus was trying to conceal his nerves. He was failing. Sent by the legate himself to oversee the retrieval of the scouts' intelligence, Severus felt the pressure of his mission.

"Centurion, what causes this delay?" Severus's voice was sharp. Falco didn't turn.

"Tribune, this forest warrants our caution," he replied, eyes still on the dark line of trees.

Falco's Optio, Varro, stepped closer, a silent shadow. Severus saw the movement and noted the way the soldiers shifted. It was a small thing, easily missed, but it was there.

"The advance scouts were sent deep to mark the stirrings of a Germanic uprising," Falco's voice was tight, "but it's something organized. A force gathering strength. The tribes are preparing. A coalition." He paused, his gaze distant. "Should we allow them the first strike? If the tribes unite, they'll have the numbers. They could strike at the Empire's heart. We're the only line standing between them and chaos."

He rubbed his brow. "Those scouts, if they managed to find the meeting points…" He trailed off. "Losing them means losing everything. We'd be stumbling forward, with nothing but shadows to guide us. If they come for us first," Falco continued, almost whispering, "it'll be like fighting a ghost."

CHAPTER 1: INTO THE FOREST

"Emperor's orders, Centurion." Severus's voice, clipped. Strained. "Hesitation? Unacceptable." He forced his shoulders back, trying to project confidence.

Severus's knuckles whitened around the reins. Tribune. Emissary of the Emperor's will. His father's ambitions—heavy like iron—wrapped tight, suffocating. Expectations that never loosened. This mission wasn't just another order; it was a trial by fire. Retrieving the scouts' intelligence was a test. Failure here wouldn't just wound his pride; it would undermine everything they'd worked to build. Yet every misstep, every disagreement with Falco, felt like another crack forming in that carefully constructed image of control. He hated the hesitation, hated that it showed. He hated how Falco's steady, unyielding tone was a quiet rebuke.

And then there was the silence—the kind that made even his thoughts sound loud. Time twisted into an adversary. His father's voice echoed: Prove yourself, or lose everything. Falco's calmness gnawed at him, a constant, unspoken comparison. Out here, hesitation wasn't just a weakness; it was an open wound.

"Emperor's orders." Severus's voice strained.

Falco's voice dipped. "This forest? Just the start. The Emperor was clear: secure the frontier, keep the tribes from uniting. If we fall short, it's not just this campaign we're losing—it's the whole northern line."

Severus shifted in his saddle, rigid. He looked ready to argue, but he didn't. Not yet. "Soldiers, Centurion. Not sheep," he spat.

There was silence. The soldiers stared ahead, some shifting slightly.

Behind Severus' back, they shared quick, wordless glances. Severus didn't notice, or maybe he refused to. But Falco caught it.

"Understood, Tribune," Falco said, his voice flat.

There was a tense pause. Then, Severus turned his horse with a frustrated tug on the reins, disappearing back down the line. Falco's gaze swept over the clearing, a silent order to keep moving.

Lucius, a veteran scout, emerged from the ranks. "Centurion," he murmured, "there are signs of an old camp just ahead. They're out there, watching, waiting."

A nod to Varro, and the signal passed quietly: stay alert, shields up. The men adjusted without a sound.

In the ranks, Titus, the youngest, couldn't help himself. "Good fortune the Tribune's mount is so wise," he whispered to Decimus, a veteran of many battles.

Decimus didn't smile. "Shut it, boy," he growled, not out of respect for the tribune, but for the silence.

The silence wasn't just the absence of sound—it was a living presence. Varro's whispered commands rippled through the ranks. Every man tightened his grip on his weapon.

Titus muttered a prayer under his breath. Next to him, Decimus's eyes darted from shadow to shadow. Falco felt the tension. He'd learned to recognize that weight in the air.

CHAPTER 1: INTO THE FOREST

The century moved on, deeper into the forest. Nearby, a young recruit named Quintus shivered. "What are we walking into?"

"Decimus," Titus's voice was barely a whisper, "how much farther?"

"You'll get your wish when we reach the clearing," Decimus said, his voice flat. "Plenty of light when the arrows start flying."

Titus forced a chuckle. "Always a cheery thought, eh?" But his words lacked their usual bite.

The century pressed onward for another mile when Falco raised his fist. The column stopped. He had spotted a clearing off the path—small, enclosed by trees. Defensible.

"We'll set up here," Falco murmured to Varro.

Varro nodded, spreading the orders. It was well into the evening, a few hours later, when they reached the clearing, the forest painted in shades of purple and gray. The place was small, but defensible. The trees pressed in on three sides. On the fourth, the path snaked back into the forest.

"Decimus," Varro called out. "Take a squad and secure that ridge."

Decimus nodded. "Titus," he said, "you're with me."

Titus managed a grin. "I wouldn't want to be a burden, old man." Decimus huffed, a small nod acknowledging the attempt at levity.

The century moved with practiced efficiency, transforming the clearing into a makeshift camp. Tents were pitched, shields stacked, and the perimeter secured. Falco locked eyes with Varro. They didn't need to speak. Falco felt the weight of their shared experience, steadying him.

Severus returned just as they were setting up. He looked ready to explode. "Centurion," he said sharply, "this is wasting time."

"The men need rest, Tribune," Falco said, his voice flat. "We fortify here; move at first light."

Severus seemed ready to argue, but relented. "Fine," he muttered, before turning away.

As Severus stalked back to his tent, Falco's gaze swept over the clearing. His men were efficient. Despite the tension with the tribune, the century trusted their centurion.

As night swallowed the clearing, twilight thickened. Falco held his ground, eyes steady on the treeline. The gladius in his hand was solid and familiar. His fingers tensed around the hilt. The quiet wasn't just quiet now. It was anticipation. It was the forest holding its breath.

Scene 1.2: Shadows Stir

As the last rays of daylight filtered through the dense canopy, the sense of safety seemed to vanish along with the light. Shadows danced and twisted in the clearing with every gust of wind, like restless spirits.

The soldiers worked quickly, their movements sharp and nearly silent, arranging their gear in tight circles, with each soldier ensuring their

CHAPTER 1: INTO THE FOREST

belongings were within arm's reach, ready to defend or move at a moment's notice. A flicker of movement in the shadows caught Falco's attention. He tensed, Gladius held low, but it was just one of his men. The recruit was new to the century, barely a man, and his eyes were wide with fear. Falco gave him a reassuring nod, and the recruit scurried away. He couldn't afford to be distracted by fear, not when their survival rested on him staying sharp. It wasn't just the plans, the tactics—they all held because of trust. Trust he couldn't let slip. Not now. Not ever.

Falco's steady voice guided them, cutting through the noise without raising it—not a whisper, but close. The clearing seemed to shrink, shadows pooling thicker as the hours crept by, as if the woods were breathing in, suffocating the space with every slow exhale. The fading light cast an eerie glow over the forest floor, making the shadows dance and the trees seem to loom closer.

A low murmur, like words just beyond reach, drifted on the wind, threading through the leaves. Falco leaned forward, straining to hear, trying to decipher the sounds. Footsteps? A rustle that shouldn't be there? Or just his mind playing tricks on him?

The forest wasn't just a backdrop—it was a predator, watching, holding its breath. Falco kept his gaze locked on the treeline, daring any shadow to move. His men felt it too; he could tell. That thick, shared tension. No one spoke; no one moved more than they had to. Every grip was tight, every breath measured, their hands resting heavy on their weapons, waiting for whatever came next.

"Perimeter tight," Falco said under his breath to Varro, his optio. "Three shifts. Pila ready."

Varro didn't speak, just dipped his head, moving to distribute the pila—the heavy Roman javelins designed to bend upon impact, preventing the enemy from throwing them back. The men knew how it worked by now—gladii within reach, shields close enough to grab in one motion. They'd learned from those who hadn't been so quick. The forest was always watching here, every rustle carrying the weight of something unseen.

"Scouts report every hour," Falco added when Varro circled back. "We're deep in now. They know we're here."

Tribune Severus stood at the camp's center, his fingers drumming a restless rhythm on the hilt of his sword. It wasn't just impatience—there was something else in that tapping, something edging close to anger. He marched toward Falco, jaw tight.

"Centurion," Severus called, his voice sharp. "Is this truly necessary? The men need rest."

Falco kept his eyes ahead, not meeting Severus's stare. "The enemy is close, Tribune."

Severus's eyes narrowed. "Caution is what's slowing us down," he muttered, gesturing at the tight lines, the poised javelins. "All of this paranoia—"

"We're in their territory," Falco interrupted, his voice low and even. "They know the woods better than we do. We make ourselves an easy target, we won't see another dawn."

Severus looked like he might snap—face tightening, pride stinging. But

CHAPTER 1: INTO THE FOREST

something about Falco's stare stopped him. He exhaled sharply, gave a curt nod, and turned away. The air felt heavier in his wake.

Titus, crouched nearby, let out a breath he'd been holding. "If we're with Pluto by dawn," he whispered to Decimus, "at least our pila will be set nice and neat."

Decimus, older and war-worn, barely spared him a glance. "Quiet, Titus," he muttered. "Eyes on the tree line."

The joke did little to ease the tension. Titus's eyes flicked nervously toward the darkness, the looming line of trees that seemed to press closer with every fading moment.

Falco walked the perimeter, checking the guards, his gaze lingering on each face. He found Varro again, standing near the edge, eyes fixed on the woods.

"Word from the scouts?" Falco asked.

"Nothing yet," Varro replied, shaking his head. "But the men are on edge. It's too quiet."

"Keep them alert," Falco muttered, his eyes following a distant shadow. He glanced back at Varro. "And keep an eye on Severus."

Varro gave a quick nod, his agreement wordless. He knew what Falco meant—tensions between leaders poisoned the ranks. Out here, it could get people killed.

The dying fire threw long, restless shadows from the center, the flames flickering like anxious fingers that couldn't quite reach the edge of the darkness. They gave off a bit of light, but no heat against the creeping night air.

The men huddled close, their whispers barely louder than the wind, as if afraid their voices might carry too far and draw something in. Lucius, ever the weathered veteran, shared a tale of a close call in Gaul, while Quintus, his eyes wide with a mix of fear and fascination, listened intently. A stale crust of bread made its way around the circle—no complaints, just hands reaching and passing it along. They'd been through worse. Always worse.

Titus, his youthful energy a stark contrast to the grim silence, spun tales of his exploits back in Rome, embellishing his stories with each telling. But his laughter felt hollow, a thin veneer over the fear that gnawed at them all.

Decimus, his face weathered and scarred, sat apart from the others, his eyes on the darkness beyond the firelight. He didn't say much—he never did—but just having him there, quiet and steady, gave the others a sense of something unbreakable. A reminder of what a Roman soldier was supposed to be.

As the night pressed in, the last remnants of light fading, Severus stepped out of his tent. He looked determined, set on something, but then he caught sight of Falco, still moving through the ranks, speaking quietly to one soldier, then the next. Severus hesitated, just for a moment, watching.

"Rest would suit you, Centurion," Severus said.

CHAPTER 1: INTO THE FOREST

"I'll rest when the men are settled," Falco replied without looking up.

Severus hesitated, then turned away, muttering something under his breath. Falco watched him go, the weight of command bearing down on both their shoulders.

Varro slipped away to join the watch, and Falco took his own post at the edge of the camp, his back against a tree. Firelight barely reached him, as if it too wanted to shrink away from the encroaching dark. Branches above rustled, muttering secrets that weren't meant for human ears. Falco crouched low, muscles tense, ears sharp. This was when it happened—always in the quiet, when even the forest seemed to hold its breath.

He'd watched soldiers unravel in these silences, break apart under the weight of waiting. The fear gnawed at him too, a constant companion that whispered doubts and painted grim possibilities in his mind. He'd learned to silence it, to push it down, to focus on the task at hand. He forced himself to breathe, to slow the frantic rhythm of his heart.

The guards were still, their eyes narrowed at the shifting shadows. Even the wind seemed hesitant, brushing through the trees softly, as if not wanting to draw attention.

Titus shifted nervously beside Decimus. "If the barbarians spare us, the Tribune's temper may yet take us down."

Decimus didn't respond, his body coiled tight. There was no room for humor here, not in the silence that felt so dense, so heavy with the threat of unseen eyes.

The cold crept in with the night air, chilling him to the bone. Falco's hand rested on his gladius, fingers tracing the worn leather grip. Every noise in the forest seemed amplified—the crack of a branch, the rustling of leaves. He stayed still, eyes fixed on the treeline, feeling the weight of the night closing in around them.

Scene 1.3: Into the Jaws

The night dragged on, thick with silence and punctuated by the occasional shuffle of boots in the watchposts—half-hearted attempts to shake off the dread that clung to everyone like a shroud. Every hour felt heavier than the last.

Falco leaned against the rough bark of the tree, tension twisting in his shoulders. Darkness crowded in, threatening to swallow them whole. Even the wind, restless and cold, seemed to skitter through the leaves, afraid to disturb the quiet. He didn't move; his eyes locked on the treeline. He waited. He listened. The silence wasn't peace, but a held breath, the kind that comes before something breaks.

With the slow creep of dawn, a pale light began to seep through the dense canopy, marking the start of a new day. The men stirred, their faces etched with exhaustion and apprehension. The night's silence had taken its toll.

Falco had been up long before the others, eyes fixed on the overgrown path. Varro approached, his voice low. "Scouts are back," he said. "Looks like they've found something."

"Bring them here," Falco replied, gaze unmoving. A knot of anxiety tightened in his gut, but he kept his voice steady.

CHAPTER 1: INTO THE FOREST

Lucius approached, saluting. "Centurion," he began, "we found signs of a struggle a few miles ahead. Broken branches, the ground churned up… and blood. Fresh blood."

Severus emerged from his tent, his voice sharp with alarm. "How fresh?"

"Within the last day, Tribune," Lucius reported.

Falco felt a chill. "Show me," he said.

They followed Lucius through the thick undergrowth, Falco pushing aside branches, his apprehension growing with each step. Finally, they reached the place where the scouts had found the signs of struggle. Falco crouched down, fingers brushing over the jagged split in a branch. "This wasn't an accident," he murmured, more to himself than anyone else. He examined the churned-up earth. "Not a chase. A path." He looked up, his gaze meeting Severus's. "They're herding us," he said, "straight into their jaws."

They retraced their steps back to the camp. Falco turned to Severus, his voice low but urgent. "Tribune," he said, "we need to proceed cautiously. There could be an ambush."

Severus's eyes flashed. "Caution?" he barked. "If we keep hesitating, we're giving them time!"

"Caution keeps men alive," Falco cut in, his voice firm. "A rushed advance could lead us right into their hands."

A murmur arose among the soldiers, who had gathered around, listening intently. Severus's fists clenched, but then he took a sharp breath. "Fine," he forced out. "But we move quickly."

Falco nodded. "Double the scouts on the flanks," he ordered Varro. "Keep the formation tight. No gaps. Shields ready."

The men adjusted their positions, weapons at the ready. Titus muttered under his breath, "The Tribune's temper might just burn our backs—assuming the enemy doesn't get to us first."

Beside him, Decimus gave a stern glance, but the look wasn't about reproach. They all felt it; the gnawing tension.

They marched on, every step a deliberate act against the fear that threatened to consume them. The forest loomed, shadows deepening. Lucius signaled a halt. Falco's instincts screamed at him to be wary.

He approached, Varro at his side. Lucius crouched, pointing to where crimson stained the leaves.

"More blood," Lucius said. "And tracks—fresh, leading deeper."

Falco's eyes caught a glint of color—fabric snagged on a branch. Roman colors. He lifted the scrap of cloth, the crimson of a Roman tunic, stained dark with blood. Severus approached, his face pale. "If they're still alive…" he whispered.

"They were taken for a reason, Tribune," Falco said. "And the enemy expects us to come charging after them."

"So you suggest we abandon them?" Severus's tone was sharp.

"No," Falco replied. "But rushing in blind does them no good either. We need to be smart."

Severus stood there, shoulders tight, fear flickering beneath his anger. He held his breath, then let it out slowly.

"Do what you must," he forced out.

Falco nodded, then turned to Varro. "Get the scouts on those tracks. We move slowly. Shields high."

Varro nodded and went to inform the others. Falco remained, scanning the treeline, senses sharp. But the woods held their silence, and the air itself felt bated.

As the line moved forward, Severus kept his voice low, his earlier bluster gone. Titus's whisper broke the silence: "It seems we march to Pluto's own gates." Decimus didn't bother replying, his eyes hard, focused on the shadows. It was no longer just unease—caution had calcified into something heavier, the awareness that each step forward might be their last.

Scene 1.4: Holding the Line

The path narrowed, snaking through the brush, swallowing the light. Branches creaked, leaves whispered, and Falco felt eyes watching— lurking just beyond sight. His hand tightened on his sword hilt. They'd held formation, shields raised, eyes scanning for the unseen, but tension thrummed through Falco's veins. "Close ranks," he muttered to the nearest soldier, voice low and taut.

Severus had demanded haste, yet here they were, moving slow as death.

A storm of arrows and spears erupted from the trees, followed by at least a hundred and fifty painted figures bursting from the undergrowth, axes and spears glinting in the dim light. Thuds and cries filled the air as iron met flesh. Marius, a young recruit, felt a chill as the man next to him crumpled, an arrow protruding from his neck. "Gods," he thought, bile rising in his throat.

"Hold!" Falco's voice cut through the chaos. Shields rose in unison, forming a wall of iron. Overlap. Scales. A wall. A spear struck, and a soldier staggered, gritting his teeth in pain.

Severus, gripped by indecision, wrestled with his horse's reins. Fight or run? His eyes darted across the battlefield, barely registering the carnage. Bodies littered the ground, the earth a churned mess of blood and mud. He shouted orders, but his voice was swallowed by the cacophony of battle. His words were lost in the brutal storm of steel on steel and the agonizing cries of his men.

Severus stood rooted to the spot, his breath catching as he took in the scene. The young recruit lay crumpled just a few steps away, a spear jutting from his thigh, the skin around it pale and strained, his mouth open in a scream that barely escaped his lips. Blood pumped out in dark, pulsing waves, pooling faster than Severus could comprehend. He wanted to move—to help, maybe?—but his body refused, locked in place by a creeping, cold fear. "Fall back!" he finally cried, but the command was a whimper, lost in the enemy's ferocious roar.

Painted figures burst from the trees, howling and whooping, axes and spears glinting in the dim light. They crashed into the Roman line with

CHAPTER 1: INTO THE FOREST

a wave of violence and fury. The ground trembled beneath their charge, and the air filled with their guttural cries.

A wave of nausea rolled over one of the seasoned legionaries as he witnessed the brutal reality of combat. A man's arm was severed, spinning through the air before landing with a sickening thud in the mud. Blood sprayed across the clearing, painting the leaves crimson. "Gods below," he gasped, steeling himself against the carnage.

Each swing of his gladius was met with bone-jarring resistance, a symphony of violence that echoed through the clearing. He saw a man's chest split open, his ribs gleaming white against the dark blood that poured out. The air was thick with the coppery stench of blood and the sharp tang of fear.

"Shields up!" Falco's voice tore through the noise. He moved like a whirlwind, deflecting a spear aimed at a terrified recruit, then burying his gladius deep into an attacker's shoulder. A scream erupted, cut short as the man fell.

Decimus, to Falco's right, fought with disciplined precision. His face was a mask of calm, his eyes cold and calculating. He parried a blow, twisted his sword, and struck with deadly efficiency.

Titus, the one who could usually make anyone laugh, fought now with a grim, almost frightening determination. He threw his pilum—a movement so practiced it was almost instinct—and it struck dead on target. No hesitation, no second guesses. Then he was moving, gladius in hand, charging forward with a force that seemed… unnatural, like he'd shed that easygoing grin along with any sense of mercy. His strikes were sharp, fierce, each one almost too focused, as if he'd buried his usual self somewhere far behind.

Severus, however, was losing control. He slid from his horse, his knees buckling as he hit the ground. The sword felt awkward in his grip. He swung wildly, nearly losing his balance.

"Severus!" Falco barked, his eyes locking onto the young tribune's shaking hands. "Help hold the line or get out of the way!"

Severus seemed to snap back to reality, nodding jerkily and stumbling towards the line. His movements were stiff and uncoordinated, his fear palpable. Falco, however, couldn't spare him more than a glance.

Varro, ever vigilant, had anticipated the enemy's flanking maneuver. "Hold the line!" he roared, directing the men into defensive positions. "Shields together! Do not break!"

Falco, his ears attuned to the rhythm of battle, heard the confidence in Varro's voice. Good. The rear would hold.

The Germanic warriors pressed their assault, their wild cries filling the air. Severus tried to rally the soldiers, but his voice was weak and ineffective. His face was pale, the futility of his commands evident as the men turned to Falco instead.

"Keep your shields locked!" Falco's voice boomed, silencing the tribune. The soldiers snapped to attention, rallying around their centurion.

The Germanic warriors sensed the momentary waver in the Roman line and surged forward again. But the Roman shields held firm, their defense unbreakable. The attackers faltered, their momentum broken against the unyielding wall of Roman shields.

Falco seized the opportunity. "Drive them back!" he roared, and the legionaries surged forward, a wave of steel and fury. The Germanic warriors, exhausted and demoralized, gave ground, stumbling back towards the treeline.

Falco, sensing victory, raised his hand. "Hold!" he commanded. The soldiers, panting and bloodied, obeyed. "Do not pursue! It's a trap."

They watched as the remaining attackers retreated, disappearing into the shadows of the forest. But Falco remained vigilant, his eyes scanning the undergrowth for any sign of another ambush. The air was heavy with anticipation, the silence unnerving.

Severus stood off to the side, his gaze fixed on the dark edge of the forest. His face was pale, his lips pressed tightly together. Falco approached him cautiously. "We need to regroup. Secure the perimeter."

Severus gave a stiff nod, his shoulders slumped under the weight of his armor and his mistakes.

Varro moved to Falco's side. "What's the plan, Centurion?"

Falco took a breath, steadying himself. "We hold this ground," he said firmly. "Tend to the wounded. Eyes open."

He glanced around, his eyes scanning the lines of trees that seemed to press in on them. "This isn't over," he muttered.

And he was right. The silence crackled with anticipation, the weight of whatever came next pressing down on them like a gathering storm.

2

Chapter 2: Signs of the Enemy

Scene 2.1: Aftermath

The day after the ambush, the century was still reeling. Soldiers moved around with wary eyes, bracing for a second blow. The metallic scent of blood mingled with the earthy aroma of decaying leaves, clinging to everything, a grim testament to the sacrifices made in the name of honor and their sworn oath to Rome. Bloodstained leaves stuck to their boots, and shards of broken shields littered the path like discarded remnants of a storm. The silence crept in, thick and smothering, as if the forest itself were holding its breath.

The sun stood high in the sky, casting a harsh light on the scene of carnage. It was midday, and they prepared to move, with a forced, practiced calm. Earlier, they had spent the morning tending to the wounded and burying the dead, and the weight of their losses hung heavy over the century. Steps were steady, eyes forward, but beneath the surface, exhaustion showed in slumped shoulders and shadowed eyes. Fear flickered in their glances, an afterimage of the ambush. The attack had exposed the clash between Roman discipline and the chaotic tactics of the Germanic tribes. It was a harsh reminder that this land wasn't theirs, not truly.

Falco moved through the ranks, his eyes lingering on the wounded. He didn't stop; he couldn't afford to. A quick nod here, a firm grip on a shoulder there—small gestures that had to suffice. Varro was already barking orders in low, measured tones, doubling the scouts' watch. They'd gotten lucky this time. Too lucky.

Falco knew their only defense now was vigilance. The enemy was out there, watching, waiting. He could feel it in the stillness of the air, in the shadows that shifted at the edge of his vision.

Severus clambered off his horse, almost stumbling, his face pale beneath his helmet. He cleared his throat, but when he spoke, his voice was barely audible.

"We... we keep going," he said, the words more a reassurance to himself than an order.

"Tribune," Falco cut him off, his voice firm but not harsh, "we proceed with caution. The fate of the scouts remains unknown."

The unspoken weight of their missing comrades settled over them. Severus shifted, concealing his trembling hands. Falco took a sharp, steadying breath.

"Form up!" he shouted, his voice slicing through the tension.

A moment of heavy silence followed, then the soldiers moved, shuffling

CHAPTER 2: SIGNS OF THE ENEMY

into line. Shields clanked together, and weapons were gripped tightly. But it was their hesitation, the lingering glances at Falco, that caught Severus's attention. It was as if they were waiting for permission, a silent defiance that made his jaw clench.

They started moving. Not marching, not anymore. It was something heavier, a silent vow to face whatever waited in the forest. And the forest watched them back, each creak and rustle a reminder of unseen eyes.

The air was thick with the coppery smell of blood and damp earth. A wave of nausea rolled over Falco, and he swallowed hard, forcing it back down. He could feel the enemy's presence, their breath mingling with the damp leaves. There was no turning back now, not with the mission driving them forward, not with their enemies demanding caution.

As they pushed another mile deeper into the thick of the forest, Falco's unease grew, the dread tightening around his chest. It felt like walking into a trap. He couldn't shake the feeling of the enemy's presence, but there was no room for retreat.

Scene 2.2: The Hunter's Snare

The forest seemed to swallow them whole. Trees, mist, and shadows closed in, pulling them deeper into the hunter's snare of the narrowing path. Each step felt like a descent.

Falco kept the ranks tight, his eyes darting between the shadows and the tangled undergrowth. The air, thick and heavy, pressed against their skin, carrying a weight beyond humidity—a tension that clung like unseen hands on their shoulders. They weren't just marching toward an enemy; they were walking into something ancient, something that breathed in the soil and rustled in the leaves. The enemy was watching, herding them—luring them deeper into the forest, away from the main force and any chance of reinforcements, towards a place where the terrain itself was a weapon in the tribes' hands.

Varro led the scouts ahead, slipping through the underbrush in near silence. Fingers tight around his gladius, he moved like a ghost, eyes sharp, ears keener. Now and then, one of the scouts would peel off from the main group, kneeling to the dirt, feeling for the smallest signs—a snapped twig, disturbed moss, the shape of footprints half-lost in mud. Quick, silent gestures passed between them, their language a dance Falco read from a distance, his unease growing with each signal.

Varro fell back to march alongside Falco, his face grim. "Recent tracks, Centurion," he reported, keeping his voice low. "Multiple groups. Campfires, still warm."

Falco nodded, his face giving nothing away, though his thoughts were racing. "Ambush?"

Varro's lips pressed together. "No signs of one. But blood—fresh. They're not hiding. They're tracking us, maybe herding us."

Falco's hand instinctively went to the pommel of his gladius. "Double the scouts," he ordered. "Fan out, flanks and rear."

Varro relayed the command, and the scouts spread out, their movements swift and silent. Falco scanned the line, his gaze lingering on Decimus. Usually unflinching, Decimus now had a tic in his jaw, his fingers drumming nervously against his shield. Even he wasn't immune to the

CHAPTER 2: SIGNS OF THE ENEMY

creeping dread.

Severus, ever impatient, pushed forward. "Why are we slowing, Centurion?" he demanded. "We're losing time."

Falco held Severus's gaze. "Fresh tracks. Blood. We need to proceed with caution."

Severus's patience was cracking. He felt the pressure of his mission, the weight of his father's expectations, and the need to prove himself. "Every rustle, every shadow—we can't hesitate for every little thing!" he exclaimed, his voice tight with the fear he was trying to suppress. "We need to move quickly, show strength, and not be deterred by imaginary threats."

"They're tracking us," Falco replied, his tone colder. "If we rush, we're blind."

Severus opened his mouth to argue, but something in Falco's voice stopped him. He recognized the Centurion's experience and the underlying warning in his tone, realizing that his own impatience might be jeopardizing the mission. He bit down on his frustration, muttering through clenched teeth, "Fine. But keep moving."

Falco turned away, feeling the weight of the men's eyes on him. Titus, ever the one to break the tension, muttered to Decimus, "It feels as though we march to Pluto's own gates."

Decimus, his gaze sweeping the dense undergrowth, didn't answer. The fear was there, plain to see in the tightness around his eyes, the way he unconsciously adjusted his grip on his pilum.

"Stay focused," Falco said, his voice sharp. "Shields up."

They pressed on. The path turned rough, strewn with hidden roots and loose stones. No birds sang, no breeze stirred the leaves. Just their breathing, loud in the eerie stillness.

The century continued its march, the tension growing with each step. As the hours passed, the sun began its descent, casting long shadows that stretched across the forest floor, mimicking the growing unease in the soldiers' hearts. As the day wore on, each step was heavier than the last. Varro, jogging back from a scouting foray, fell into step beside Falco once more. "More tracks, Centurion," he reported, his voice strained. "More of them. Moving faster."

The chill Falco felt earlier settled deeper. They weren't just being watched; they were being led.

The forest thickened, closing in like a suffocating fist. The air grew heavy with the scent of damp earth and decaying leaves, and the silence was broken only by the occasional drip of water and the rustle of unseen creatures in the undergrowth. Branches overhead twisted, blocking the weak sunlight, turning their path into a dim tunnel. The soldiers, their bodies weary from the long march, trudged onwards, their minds filled with thoughts of the unseen dangers lurking in the shadows. Every snap of a twig, every rustle of leaves, every creak of leather, felt like a breath on their necks.

Titus, his voice barely a whisper, said to Decimus, "You think the tribes know every move we make?"

Decimus remained silent, his hand hovering over the pommel of his

CHAPTER 2: SIGNS OF THE ENEMY

gladius. But his silence spoke volumes.

A sharp crack—branches snapping nearby. Falco's hand shot up, signaling the column to halt. Shields rose, weapons were readied. Severus started forward, but Falco silenced him with a glare.

The men stood motionless, the only sound the rustling of leaves and their own ragged breathing. The scouts fanned out, searching for the source of the disturbance. They returned moments later, shaking their heads. No sign of anything.

"Onward—for the gods and Rome!" Falco barked, his voice firm, though his stomach churned. "Eyes open, ears alert. Stay sharp."

The column pressed forward, quieter now, the silence wrapping around them like a shroud. Falco knew they were stepping deeper into a trap, but there was no turning back.

Scene 2.3: March of Tension

The sun was beginning its descent as the afternoon wore on, casting long, dancing shadows across the forest floor. After another hour of cautious marching, covering a mile, the pass opened slightly, thick shadows pooled between trunks and tangled roots, swallowing the legionaries whole. It was the kind of quiet that gnawed at nerves, where every leaf rustled with the threat of ambush, every snapping twig a whispered warning.

Footfalls were muffled by moss and decaying leaves; the only sounds were the creak of leather, the clink of armor, and the rasp of breaths held too long. Falco, at the head of the century, scanned the woods restlessly. A cold dread coiled in his gut. The disturbances were too frequent: broken branches, churned earth where no boot should have trod—telltale signs of the enemy's presence, their movements deliberate and calculated.

Severus, however, was right on his heels, a man clearly devoid of patience today. The tribune reined in his horse, fingers knotted tight around the leather reins. His eyes, sharp and irritated, betrayed the restlessness simmering beneath his disciplined facade.

Scouts had returned with signs: fresh tracks, the ghostly remnants of smoke, lingering warmth on old fire pits. But this forced inactivity twisted Severus's insides with a desperate urgency. They were losing time—losing it to the encroaching shadows and Falco's caution.

"Centurion!" Severus's voice cut through the stillness, sharp enough to make the nearest men flinch. "This crawl is intolerable. We need to move."

"Tribune," Falco countered, his voice carrying down the line, "we should send out more scouts to sweep ahead, ensure—"

"There's no time," Severus cut him off, voice tight, eyes narrowed.

"Every moment we hesitate gives them more time to regroup, to reinforce," Falco insisted, the ranks of men behind him a silent, watchful presence.

Falco inhaled slowly, released the breath through his nose. "Tribune, if we rush in—"

CHAPTER 2: SIGNS OF THE ENEMY

"Enough!" Severus's word cracked like a whip, his face taut with fury.

Falco's jaw tightened, but he gave a curt nod, stepping back. Open defiance here would only ripple through the men like a disease—doubt, fear, a collapse of order. He couldn't allow it. Not with so many lives depending on him.

As Severus urged his horse forward, Falco's eyes met Varro's. The optio wore his usual unreadable expression—was he waiting for Falco to push back harder, or silently calculating the risks?

"Double the scouts," Falco murmured.

Varro nodded and vanished into the ranks, a wraith among the legionaries. The air grew heavy, pressing down on them with the weight of anticipation. Every man felt it, like a bowstring pulled taut, threatening to snap.

Titus, somewhere in the middle of the formation, muttered through clenched teeth, "Marching straight into Hades, and we're just whistling a merry tune."

Decimus, a few paces ahead, didn't even glance his way. His jaw was set, eyes searching the dark walls of foliage. Falco felt the unease rippling through the ranks—soldiers subtly raising their shields, the tremor in their hands as they gripped their spears. They were waiting, bracing for the inevitable.

The path narrowed, branches bending inward like closing jaws, the forest seeming to close in around the century. No wind stirred the leaves, but the silence was a living thing, pressing in on them, watching, waiting. Falco felt Severus draw up beside him again, felt the man's impatience radiating like heat.

"You hesitate, Centurion," Severus said, his frustration clear.

"My only concern is for the safety of these men, Tribune," Falco replied, voice clipped. He didn't want this to escalate, not here, not now. But the warning in his tone was unavoidable. "The enemy is close."

"I am in command here, Falco." Severus's voice had an edge; his authority had been tested too many times today. "And I will not tolerate insubordination."

"Understood, Tribune," Falco said, weighing each word. He needed to extinguish this spark before it ignited a wildfire that consumed the entire column. But Severus's silence only fueled the tension. He barked a final order, louder than necessary, as if trying to drown out the doubts simmering beneath the surface. "We press on. No more delays."

When the march resumed, Falco could almost taste the tension, bitter and acrid. Even Titus, always ready with a sardonic quip, remained silent, his jaw locked.

Varro materialized beside him, his voice barely audible over the tramp of boots on the forest floor. "Movement ahead," he murmured. "Can't make out numbers yet."

"Tell the scouts to stay sharp," Falco replied, eyes fixed on the path. "And keep a close watch on Severus."

A nod, and Varro melted back into the ranks. Falco took a breath,

CHAPTER 2: SIGNS OF THE ENEMY

forcing his shoulders to relax, even as his instincts blared at him that this was a mistake, that they needed to stop, to—

Movement ahead. A scout signaled, hand raised—halt. Falco's own hand rose in response, the century snapping to a standstill. Weapons shifted, eyes darted, the men taut, poised on the edge of a precipice.

Severus pushed forward, demanding answers. "Why have we stopped?" he barked, his voice echoing through the trees.

"Movement ahead, Tribune," Falco replied, low and firm. "We should proceed cautiously—"

"We cannot afford to stop for every—" Severus's voice cracked with impatience. "Press forward!"

"Tribune, if we—"

"Enough!" Severus's face flushed, his voice booming through the ranks. Every man held his breath, the silence amplifying the tribune's fury. Severus fixed Falco with a glacial stare. "We move, now!"

A long silence stretched. Falco held Severus's gaze, weighing his options, the lives of his men hanging in the balance. Then, with a slow nod, he said, his voice flat, devoid of emotion, "As you command, Tribune."

Severus wheeled his horse around. The soldiers lurched forward, their movements stiff and mechanical, the cohesion of the century fractured by doubt. Falco's mind raced, trying to anticipate, to pierce the shadows, but he saw nothing. He felt the inevitability of what was to come, the ambush coiled just out of sight.

The century pressed on, every rustle a harbinger of danger. Falco's grip on his gladius tightened, knuckles bone-white, his breath shallow and rapid. He knew what waited in the shadows, felt it in his bones.

And they were marching straight towards it.

Scene 2.4: Marching into the Jaws

The column pushed on, swallowed by shadows and the thickening air; every man wound tight like a drawn bowstring. The narrow path seemed to stretch endlessly, each step dragging them deeper into a dark maze of trees and tangled underbrush. Falco's breaths were measured, but every part of him was ready to snap. His eyes swept the treeline in restless arcs—there, then gone, only to whip back again at the faintest flicker of movement.

Varro kept close, his usual calm masking a growing sense of dread. He didn't speak; he just adjusted his grip on his shield and checked the men behind him. It wasn't words that held the century together now—it was silence, stretched thin and cracking at the edges.

Behind them, Severus sat stiffly in his saddle, his lips a thin line of irritation. His impatience rippled through the ranks, sharpening the soldiers' unease. To Severus, this march was a test of control, not survival. And that made him dangerous in all the wrong ways. Varro knew it, and so did Falco, but what could they do? Not here, not now, not in front of the men.

It was Titus, ever the grumbler, who broke the silence first—just loud enough for Decimus to hear. "This isn't marching," he muttered, his fingers tapping anxiously on the worn grip of his sword. "This is a

CHAPTER 2: SIGNS OF THE ENEMY

goddamned funeral procession."

Decimus didn't answer. Just stared hard into the gloom, his jaw set. Words wouldn't help now.

Up ahead, the scout reappeared, moving quickly but deliberately, eyes darting over his shoulder as if he expected something to lunge from the dark. He stopped short of Falco and whispered in a voice that barely hid its urgency, "They're coordinating—groups, weapons drawn. Signals passing between them."

Falco felt the chill sink into his bones, a warning he couldn't ignore. It settled deep, like something bad waiting to happen. He turned to Varro. "Hold the line," he ordered, keeping his voice firm but low, as if saying it louder would tempt the cold into something worse. "Reinforce the flanks—double the watch."

Severus had already caught sight of the scout. The impatience was written all over him. He spurred his horse closer, barely reigning it in, like he might just bolt off himself. "What now?" he demanded, voice sharp and cutting.

Falco didn't flinch. "We've got a larger force ahead, Tribune. Moving in coordination. We should halt and reassess before proceeding."

Severus's eyes flashed, his hands twitching on the reins. "Halt?" he scoffed, louder than he needed to. "The longer we wait, the tighter their noose becomes. You're letting fear rule your judgment, Centurion."

There it was again—that tone, that blind insistence. Falco held his gaze steady, almost detached. "If we move forward without a clear picture, we risk the entire column, Tribune."

"We risk more by doing nothing!" Severus barked, anger flaring in his eyes. "You forget your place, Centurion."

Falco's expression didn't change. "My place," he said, each word careful and deliberate, "is ensuring these men survive."

For a heartbeat, it looked like Severus might lash out, but something held him back. Pride, maybe, or the thin thread of authority he felt slipping from his grasp. His jaw worked silently for a moment before he turned away with a jerk of the reins. "We continue," he snapped over his shoulder. "No more delays."

Falco exhaled slowly. Arguing now would only break their ranks, split the command, and he couldn't let that happen. "As you command," he murmured, the words bitter in his mouth.

And so they moved forward, a slow, heavy march into the wolf's jaws. Shields clutched tighter, breaths held longer. Varro gave quiet orders, firming up the line, while Falco remained at the front, eyes scanning, muscles coiled. Every rustle was a breath held too long; every shadow seemed to deepen, stretching thin the fraying nerves of every soldier in the line.

Minutes crawled by, until another scout appeared—face pale, eyes wide. He hurried to Falco, his voice hushed but urgent. "Larger numbers, all around us. Heavily armed. They're signaling each other."

Falco's heartbeat pounded in his ears, like it was trying to escape. This wasn't just some random skirmish—no, this was a trap, carefully

CHAPTER 2: SIGNS OF THE ENEMY

planned. "Hold here," he barked, a little louder than intended. "Prepare for a confrontation."

The century closed ranks, shields lifting in unison, overlapping like scales on some iron beast. Breaths came fast and shallow. Ragged. Falco glanced over his shoulder and saw Severus striding up, eyes blazing, fury etched into every tight line of his face. Veins bulged at his temples, almost as if they were about to burst. He was ready to explode, it seemed—again.

"Why have we stopped?" Severus demanded, his voice quivering with impatience.

Falco met his eyes without flinching. "We're surrounded, Tribune. A larger force—organized. If we push on now, we'll walk straight into their ambush."

Severus's face flushed red, a bead of sweat trickling down his temple. "We cannot afford to stop!" he spat, his voice climbing in pitch. "If we wait, they'll close in completely!"

Falco stood firm, his tone unyielding. "If we press on blindly, Tribune, we won't just be surrounded—we'll be slaughtered."

Severus's fists clenched and unclenched. His voice was strained, almost desperate now. "I am the one in command here! You will follow my orders!"

Falco's eyes didn't waver. "My duty is to protect these men," he said, low and steady, each word a thinly veiled defiance.

Severus seemed to teeter on the edge of a decision, his face tight with frustration and something else—something close to fear. "No more delays," he forced out, almost a whisper. "We continue."

Falco knew there was nothing more to be said. He nodded, the gesture empty. "As you command, Tribune."

The column pushed on, each step a dull drumbeat against the oppressive silence. Falco's eyes flicked to Varro—no words were exchanged, but the meaning was clear. Be ready.

The forest swallowed them whole, shadows closing in like a vice. Ahead, the path narrowed, overgrown with tangled roots and brambles. And then came the rustling—more frequent now, more deliberate. Every man's grip tightened on his weapon. Every breath came faster, shallower.

Falco's hand found his gladius, his fingers curling around the worn hilt. He could hear the blood pounding in his ears and feel the eyes watching them from the dark. The column moved forward into the waiting jaws, and Falco knew the next moment would bring violence, chaos, and blood.

It was just a matter of when.

Scene 2.5: Doubt in the Ranks

The narrow path seemed to stretch forever, like it had no end—closing in tighter with every step. Towering trees loomed, their dense branches and tangled underbrush feeling more like walls than forests, cutting off daylight and drowning them in shadow. Severus rode near the

CHAPTER 2: SIGNS OF THE ENEMY

front, stiff in the saddle, eyes darting with every rustle of leaves, every crack in the undergrowth. An enemy he couldn't see but knew was there—watching, waiting.

Falco led the century with tight discipline. Silent gestures with Varro kept the men in a solid formation. Varro moved like a shadow between them, eyes scanning, reinforcing their readiness with quick glances. Tension rippled through the ranks, an unease that spread silently. Everyone felt it—something was coming.

Suddenly, movement ahead. Falco's hand shot up, a silent command. The column froze. Shields and gladii clutched tighter, breaths held. Scouts motioned from the front—something in the underbrush, they signaled. Falco's face hardened, eyes combing the tree line.

Varro was at his side in an instant. His voice barely a murmur: "The scouts report movement ahead. They're not sure of the numbers—but it looks organized. Waiting."

Falco didn't hesitate. He turned to Severus, who looked like he was wrestling with his own fear. "Tribune, we should halt and reassess," Falco said, voice low. "The scouts' reports—"

Severus's eyes narrowed, and his frustration broke through, spilling out louder than intended. "We don't have time for this, Falco!" He snapped. A few soldiers shifted uncomfortably, the tension feeding off their leaders' exchange. "If we stop now, we'll be surrounded!"

Falco's tone stayed steady. "Tribune, moving forward without knowing what's ahead could lead us straight into a trap. We need confirmation."

"Overly cautious, Centurion!" Severus's voice strained with every word, rising defensively. His eyes darted, aware of the watching soldiers. "I'm in command, and I say we move!"

The divide was stark now. The soldiers felt it. Titus, murmuring to Decimus, "Feels like we're walking into a wolf's den."

Decimus just stared ahead, face tight. The men's fingers tightened around their weapons, breaths shallow, waiting for the next word to tip the balance.

"Tribune," Falco said, voice firm but not insubordinate, "the signs—"

"I gave you an order!" Severus's voice broke, louder than ever. His knuckles were white on the reins, anger and fear fighting for control. "We move forward. Now."

It hung there. An unspoken challenge. Falco held Severus's gaze. Disobeying a direct order meant crossing a line. But obeying could mean death for all of them. He opened his mouth to speak—Varro stepped forward, voice soft, almost a whisper. "Centurion, perhaps we could send a few more scouts? Just to confirm the way?"

Severus's face was flushed, rage and indecision churning behind his eyes. He knew it was risky to refuse Varro outright—it would shatter what remained of his authority. His lips pressed together, words fighting to break free. "Fine," he spat, barely audible. "But be quick about it."

Falco nodded once, a sharp acknowledgment to Varro, who moved instantly, signaling the scouts to advance. The men held their ground, eyes on the dark, foreboding underbrush. Silence thickened, every

CHAPTER 2: SIGNS OF THE ENEMY

snapped twig or rustling leaf a reminder of how close danger lay.

The scouts returned, faces pale. Lucius, an old veteran, spoke in a low, urgent voice, "Bodies. Roman scouts. Slain and hidden in the brush. Signs of a larger force ahead—they're getting ready."

Severus turned white as death. His hands trembled on the reins, his mouth working to find words that didn't come. He didn't just miss the signs—they'd been watching all along. Waiting. Preparing.

Falco's face remained hard, unreadable. He turned to Varro. "Double the scouts on the flanks. Stay sharp."

Varro moved like a man on a mission, issuing orders swiftly and efficiently. Severus stood, frozen in place. The reality of it all had sunk in—his authority was a thin thread now, unraveling fast.

"Centurion…" Severus started, his voice barely a whisper. "We should—"

"We need to secure the area," Falco cut in, voice calm, firm, but carrying weight. "Prepare for another attack."

Severus nodded, eyes blank. Shoulders slumped, and he turned away. Soldiers exchanged knowing glances. Their trust had shifted, the unspoken truth clear: Severus's grip on command was gone, and Falco had quietly taken the helm.

Varro approached, his expression grim. "More movement reported. We should reinforce the perimeter."

Falco gave a single nod. "Do it."

The air was heavy; every breath labored under the forest's oppressive quiet. Varro moved with purpose, orders sharp and to the point. Falco took a moment to scan the line—dead, wounded, but still standing. Always moving forward.

Severus stood off to the side, eyes lowered, mouth tight with whatever words were choking him. Falco approached, voice low. "Tribune, we must stay focused. They're still watching us."

Severus swallowed hard. His face was pale, trying to find strength in the midst of his failure. "Yes," he managed, barely above a murmur. "Of course."

And so the soldiers braced themselves once more, knowing this wasn't over. The forest pressed in, as dark and silent as a hunter's breath. Falco could feel the weight of command settle on his shoulders, a burden that came with knowing what must be done—and how fragile a line they all walked now.

3

Chapter 3: The Scattered Intelligence

Scene 3.1: Recovering the Documents

The sun had risen and set once since the century's entry into the forest, marking the beginning of the second day. Yet, the forest still held its breath around them. Each day felt like an eternity, the constant threat of attack weighing heavily on the soldiers.

Falco and his century moved like shadows along a narrowing path. The underbrush loomed thick, every rustle amplifying their sense of exposure.

At the front, Falco held firm, knowing the men watched him for every sign. They trusted Falco because he'd stood with them in the trenches, sharing their scars and carrying a few of their ghosts.

Too many lives relied on his judgment. Each decision felt like rolling dice with those familiar faces etched on every side—a gamble with lives he couldn't afford to lose. He buried the doubt deep, leaving no room for hesitation.

Most days, the weight felt relentless, pressing down even though Falco wasn't carrying it alone. The men looked at him like he was holding their world together, dread lingering behind their eyes. And beside him, Varro was there—silent and unshakable, a steady shadow where words weren't needed.

"Eyes open," Varro's voice cut through the silence, low and steady.

"Remember where we are."

Still, even with Varro's shadow keeping pace, the weight of command crept up like the tide. Slow, relentless. Swallowing things, bit by bit. He could almost feel it around his ankles—cold and heavy. If he went under, the others would go down with him. He'd seen it before. Hell, watched men lose their grip right when they needed it most. Good men. Not him, though. He couldn't let that happen. Not now. There was too much tangled up in every choice: families waiting back home, barely breathing between letters; faces of comrades who'd laid their trust in him. Each decision felt like holding a blade by its edge—balancing it just right so it didn't cut through everything he was fighting to protect.

The pressure was relentless. No room to pause, not even a breath. If he slipped—just once—it'd all break apart. Trust, gone. Like a thread snapping, and then? They'd all be falling down into the dark.

Behind him, Severus walked stiffly, the memory of the dead scouts still lingering like a shadow across his face. Falco could see it in the young tribune's eyes—the effort to hold it together. He hadn't said a word since they'd learned about the enemy movements. Not out of discipline,

CHAPTER 3: THE SCATTERED INTELLIGENCE

but fear. It was a fear that ran deeper than the threat of the Germanic tribes; it was the fear of his own inadequacy, the realization that he might not be the leader he'd always believed himself to be.

Severus fought to keep his hands steady, gripping the hilt of his sword as if it might ground him. He had trained for this, studied the scrolls of strategy and tactics, but none of it had prepared him for this relentless silence, the constant dread of knowing the enemy could be watching and planning. And with every glance at Falco, he saw his own inadequacies, an unspoken judgment from a man who seemed carved from iron while Severus's nerves felt like brittle wood. That resentment was growing like a weed in his chest, twisting tighter with every decision Falco made without hesitation, without asking for Severus's approval.

The young tribune wanted to speak up, to show he was in charge, but every time he tried, the words just—died. It was like staring into a reflection that no longer matched the image he held of himself, a growing dissonance that chipped away at his confidence.

The silence didn't help. It made everything louder—the doubts, the fear creeping up his spine, the whispers of the men who looked to Falco for reassurance. Each glance, each hesitant step, was a wordless indictment of his leadership, a silent accusation that he couldn't ignore. Severus felt bare, like everyone could see straight through him. He needed to break it, say something, and prove himself, but the words still stuck, caught in his throat by the weight of his own self-doubt. It was a new sensation for Severus, this feeling of inadequacy, and it gnawed at him with a ferocity that rivaled the fear he felt of the Germanic tribes.

Varro moved among the ranks, a whisper of reassurance as he adjusted their formation. Shields rose, the soft thud echoing in the tense quiet as every man scanned for movement, expecting the enemy to come hurtling from the shadows.

The forest breathed, almost waiting. Too quiet, too careful—each rustle in the undergrowth, setting their nerves on edge. After hours of following a clear trail, the terrain became deceptive, and the dense foliage made it difficult to stay on track. Falco's unease grew with every step, the feeling of being watched intensifying.

The air itself felt heavy, charged with anticipation. Falco's senses were on high alert, every instinct screaming at him that they were walking into a trap.

Then the path opened into a clearing, and Falco's hand shot up. The century froze. Tense silence. Falco signaled Varro, who nodded and handpicked a few scouts to sweep ahead. The rest held, breaths shallow, muscles coiled.

Titus, ever the cynic, leaned in toward Decimus and muttered, "Feels like we're walking into a tomb." Decimus said nothing, his eyes still sweeping the treeline. Better to keep that fear to yourself.

An unnerving quiet blanketed the clearing. Just the occasional caw of some far-off crow cutting through the silence. Sunlight tried to reach in, sure, but it was like the beams decided to steer clear, leaving the place wrapped in its usual, stubborn gloom.

When Varro came back, he didn't need to say much; Falco could read it on his face. But Varro spoke anyway, his voice barely above a whisper. "There was a struggle," he muttered. "Gear scattered, weapons snapped, and bodies." Falco studied the clearing. It was a place of death, a brutal

CHAPTER 3: THE SCATTERED INTELLIGENCE

testament to the fight that had happened here. The silence was heavy, filled with the ghosts of the fallen, their whispers echoing through the trees. He forced himself to look at the others. They were all tense, jaws set, eyes flicking nervously—scared but ready. Ready enough, at least.

"Secure the perimeter," Falco ordered, voice barely above a whisper. "No sudden moves. Stay sharp."

The soldiers moved with practiced efficiency, but you could tell—they were uneasy. It wasn't obvious—more like something you felt in the way their eyes flicked over dark corners. They'd been in tight spots before, tough ones, but this time felt different. The silence was thicker, heavier, like the air itself was waiting for something to break. And the shadows—yeah, those seemed deeper somehow, more like they were hiding things instead of just being shadows. Then there was the weight of the dead, too, pressing in on them—that invisible heaviness that clung to the back of your neck, no matter what you did to shrug it off.

Falco's gaze drifted along the line, taking in each man's face like he was scanning pages in some old, half-forgotten book—one he wasn't sure he wanted to finish reading. The twitch of a finger. Face set like flint. And there was the slightest shuffle, as if trying to hide behind their shields without really moving. He knew this wasn't fear. They'd met fear on other fields, stared it down, and broken it like a poorly made sword.

But this—this was worse. Doubt. The kind that seeps in, slow and insidious, like water finding its way through cracked stone. Whispering at the edges of his thoughts, saying everything might just collapse if even one of them slipped. Just one wrong step, and the whole line would come apart, trained men turning into a panicked mess, running and shouting, no sense or order left.

Falco couldn't let that happen. Not here, not now.

He had to be the anchor, unyielding while everything else wavered. Even as the trees seemed to close in, shadows creeping long like fingers reaching from old graves, he couldn't let his own unease show. Couldn't let them see that the shadows looked to him like every past failure, waiting to rise again and pull them under.

He took a deep breath, steadying himself. He was the Centurion. Their leader. He wouldn't let them down.

Varro passed on the orders, and the soldiers spread out, not exactly in a clean line but enough to surround the clearing. Quiet slipped back in, only interrupted now and then by a rustle in the leaves or a distant birdcall. It was like the whole forest was waiting, holding its breath. Falco couldn't shake the tension twisting in his gut—tightening like a fist. He had a bad feeling about this. A really bad feeling. Like they were missing something. Or maybe something was waiting for them to mess up.

Falco led a few men forward into the clearing. The ground was a mess—torn earth, blood stains, crumpled bits of armor. A smoldering campfire sat in the middle, barely alive. There had been a fight here, a desperate one. Severus followed reluctantly, his face ashen. His knuckles whitened around the hilt of his sword, but he didn't speak, and Falco didn't waste time asking for his thoughts. Not now.

"Search the area," Falco commanded, his voice sharp. "Find anything that might tell us what happened here." The men moved carefully, their

CHAPTER 3: THE SCATTERED INTELLIGENCE

eyes scanning the wreckage, their fingers tracing the bloodstains and the broken weapons. The air was thick with the scent of death and decay, a grim reminder of the price of conflict, not just in lives lost but in the erosion of a way of life. The Germanic tribes' freedom was slowly chipped away by the relentless Roman war machine.

Falco kneeled by the half-collapsed tent, fingers brushing through broken bits of armor and scraps of torn parchment. Varro came up beside him. Neither had to speak at first—just a quick, knowing look passed between them, the kind that carried too much weight.

"They made their stand here," Varro muttered, voice low and rough. "Didn't stand a chance."

"Looks like they were trying to protect something," Titus said, pointing at a mess of scattered documents. "Maybe they managed to hide some of it."

Decimus knelt, fingers brushing over the dirt as he studied the ground. He grunted. "Doesn't matter now," he muttered, voice tight. "They're gone, and if we don't find what we need—" he glanced around like the shadows were listening. "We're next."

Titus's usual cheer faltered, the weight of Decimus's words hitting him like a punch. He looked at the fallen scouts, their faces frozen in a mask of terror, and a shiver ran down his spine.

The signs of struggle were plain enough—broken weapons, bits of armor tossed around, the earth churned up where men had made their last stands. He took in the sight—scattered bodies, all caught in their final moments, as if they'd tried to form a circle, a desperate attempt to hold.

The enemy had ripped through them like a storm, or maybe something worse. Something relentless. Nothing was left untouched.

Quintus, his voice trembling slightly, held up a crumpled object. "Found this," he said, his voice barely above a whisper, as if afraid to break the silence that held the weight of their discovery.

Falco took the parchment, moving slowly, almost gingerly, not wanting to tear it more than it already was. It turned out to be a letter—a rushed warning from the scouts, scrawled in uneven lines and blotched with dark, dried blood. It spoke of a coalition—Germanic tribes banding together, planning something big, a coordinated attack. But the rest? Falco frowned. The details were cut off abruptly, half-formed sentences trailing into nothing, like the writer hadn't had enough time—or maybe air—to finish.

"Varro," Falco said, barely loud enough to be heard, "gather any other documents you can find. We're missing pieces."

Varro moved fast, urging a more thorough sweep. Soldiers combed through the remnants, their hands sinking into blood and dirt. Not far off, Severus kept his distance, eyes locked on the fallen scouts. He stood there, almost like he was trying to piece it all together—death, command, the choices that had dragged them to this point. A mess of decisions, maybe. Or just the one bad call.

Falco glanced over and caught Severus's eye. Saw the turmoil. "This intel's everything," Falco said, voice low but tight. "We can't leave until we find it all."

CHAPTER 3: THE SCATTERED INTELLIGENCE

Severus swallowed, the words coming out thin. "They died for this," he muttered, staring down at the scouts like he owed them more. "We can't let their deaths be in vain."

"We won't," Falco replied firmly, meeting Severus's gaze.

"But we need to stay focused. The enemy's still watching."

Falco's gaze swept over the clearing, taking in the carnage. The scattered bodies of his men, their faces frozen in a mask of fear and determination. He clenched his jaw, swallowing the grief that kept bubbling up. He couldn't afford to lose it now. The search turned up more fragments—maps, letters, scraps that felt like a jigsaw with missing corners. Not the whole picture, no, but enough to grasp the scale of what was coming.

Varro handed the papers to Falco, who flipped through them fast, piecing bits together with practiced eyes. He nodded more to himself than anyone else. They had confirmation of the threat but not the full plan. The missing intelligence loomed over them like a shadow.

"We have enough to know what we're up against," Falco murmured to Varro, "but not enough to stop it. We need the rest."

Falco's mind raced. Where was the missing intelligence? How could they get to it before it was too late? He exchanged a look with Varro, who understood the urgency without a word needing to be said.

"Prepare the men," Falco ordered, his voice sharp.

"We move forward."

The soldiers regrouped, moving with the mechanical efficiency of men who knew no other way than forward. Severus stayed silent, head bowed, shoulders tense. Falco watched him struggle, fearing a palpable tension in the young man's frame. He took one last look at the clearing, the bodies of the scouts lying still and broken. A heavy silence pressed down.

Their deaths had bought them time, but at a cost he could feel gnawing at the edges of his resolve. Then he turned, facing the path ahead.

The forest closed in around them as the century resumed its march, every step marked by the weight of what they carried—grief, dread, and the burden of duty. Falco walked at the front, eyes sharp, senses on edge. The enemy was out there, hidden in the shadows, waiting.

And the path ahead wasn't getting any wider.

Scene 3.2: Pressing Forward

The forest loomed, the shadows deepening like the trees were leaning in, watching. And maybe they were. It wasn't just silent here; it was heavy—something alive almost, a weight that pressed in from every side. No one said more than they had to, and when they did, it was in these low, careful whispers, like talking too loud would shatter whatever held the place together. Even breathing felt risky, like you might wake something up that didn't want to be disturbed.

Falco kept his eyes straight ahead, every muscle tense, fighting against the sense that the forest itself was watching. Varro was a shadow at his back, eyes scanning the treeline, his gladius an extension of his will. He moved with a practiced calm, but his jaw was tight, a testament to the

CHAPTER 3: THE SCATTERED INTELLIGENCE

tension coiling inside.

Severus rode silently, hands locked on the reins as if they were the only thing keeping him in the saddle. He didn't look so sure of himself anymore. Not after the scouts. Not after seeing the half-burned papers in that abandoned camp. It was sinking in now, like a stone in deep water. He kept glancing at Falco, watching the way the centurion moved with that cold, precise efficiency. And each glance came with a frown that seemed caught somewhere between resentment and a grim sort of respect.

Only Titus dared break the silence. "What do you think, Decimus?" he muttered, just loud enough for his friend to hear. "Think the tribes have a nice warm welcome waiting for us?" Decimus didn't acknowledge the question, his focus fixed on the thick underbrush, but the way his fingers tightened around the hilt of his gladius spoke volumes.

The soldiers pressed forward, the line moving like one tense creature. Every so often, Falco signaled a scout to break off and slip into the underbrush. A hand raised, a nod, no words exchanged. They moved with the silence of ghosts. Varro approached, his voice barely a whisper, "Men are holding steady."

Falco nodded, eyes still locked ahead. "Good. But stay sharp," he murmured. "They're close." The air crackled with anticipation. Minutes dragged by, each one an eternity. One of the scouts returned, moving with an urgency that set Falco's nerves on edge. He leaned in close, his voice low. "The path's clear, but… there are signs of movement. Tracks. Broken branches."

Falco didn't flinch, his expression unreadable. "We move," he said, his voice low and steady. "Double the watch on the flanks. Keep it tight." The scout nodded, and a flicker of understanding passed between Falco and Varro. They were playing a losing hand, but they had no other choice.

The forest pressed in, the shadows deepening, and the air grew heavy with anticipation. The column resumed, and now every man was walking with a tightness in his shoulders that spoke of coiled nerves and thoughts best left unsaid.

Severus watched Falco; his gaze hardened. There was a hunger in his gaze, a desperate need to assert himself. He urged his horse forward, breaking the rhythm of the march. "We should alter our route, Centurion," he said, his voice tight. Falco didn't even turn. "Leaving the path would leave us exposed," he replied calmly.

"We stick to the route."

Frustration flashed across Severus's face, just for a second. He looked like he wanted to argue, but there was something in the way Falco held himself—quiet, steady—that made Severus pause. Intimidated, maybe. Instead of fighting it, he gave a stiff nod, retreating a step as if trying to hold onto whatever authority he had left. But the soldiers noticed. They always noticed these things. And now, an unspoken question lingered: who was really in charge here?

Titus leaned towards Decimus again, his voice dripping with bitter amusement. "Tribune's starting to see it, huh? Writing on the wall."

Decimus didn't say a word, didn't even glance over. He didn't need to. There was a readiness in the set of his jaw, a vigilance that spoke volumes.

They pressed on, the path growing tighter, the trees almost close enough to touch. The soldiers walked with shields high, every step slow and deliberate. And then, suddenly, a scout came running back, face pale, breathing hard. Falco turned, eyes narrowing. The scout leaned in, speaking fast and quiet. "Movement up ahead. Armed figures in the trees—multiple groups."

Falco's eyes hardened. His voice, when he spoke, was sharp and steady. "Hold the column. Prepare for engagement."

Varro was already moving, relaying orders with the precision of someone who's done it a hundred times before. Shields tightened. Gladii were drawn. Eyes locked on the treeline, trying to pierce through the shadows and catch a glimpse of what waited. Severus rode forward, forcing what looked like a mask of calm onto his face. "What's happening?" he demanded, his voice pitched higher than he intended.

"The scouts report enemy movements, Tribune," Falco replied, voice measured, almost too steady. "We're holding until we confirm their numbers."

Severus's face went red—a mix of anger and something that looked a lot like fear. "We can't keep stopping every time a branch rustles!" he snapped.

Falco's gaze met his, unyielding. "If we move forward without confirmation, we risk walking into an ambush," he said quietly, but the weight of his words made it clear it wasn't a suggestion.

Severus wanted to lash out, to demand something, but the reality of the situation kept his tongue tied. He turned sharply, riding back to his place. Titus let out a low, grim chuckle. "Marching right into the wolf's jaws, and we're just whistling along," he muttered to Decimus.

The silence pressed in, heavy and expectant. Falco motioned for the scouts to spread out and cover the flanks. They moved with practiced silence, but the shadows seemed to watch them, waiting for them to make a mistake. They just didn't know when it would strike.

Scene 3.3: The Coordinated Attack

The soldiers advanced with a slow, deliberate caution, shields held high and eyes flicking towards every rustle.

The narrow pass funneled them between towering trees, the dense forest crowding in from all sides. Falco stayed out front, taking point with slow, deliberate steps—measured and careful, like he was testing the ground for traps. It was too quiet, and the silence? It pressed in harder than the trees did. Now and then, a branch creaked or some far-off bird let out a sharp call, but otherwise, nothing. Just dark shapes where trees twisted and tangled together, their branches clawing at what little light managed to break through. It felt more like a tunnel than a path. A winding, dark throat leading them deeper and deeper into enemy territory.

Varro, moving deftly along the ranks, kept the line tight—almost too tight.

He signaled, a quick flick of the fingers, and the men braced their shields. They had seen the enemy too—fleeting shadows moving between the

CHAPTER 3: THE SCATTERED INTELLIGENCE

trees. An organized force, waiting and watching. "If the wolves don't get us," Titus muttered to Decimus, "their brothers will." Decimus didn't respond, his gaze fixed on the dark treeline, his fingers flexing over his gladius hilt.

The others shifted uneasily, exchanging glances that spoke louder than words. Doubt was like a shadow hanging over them all, feeding off the silence.

Severus rode towards the center of the column, but his grip on the reins was too tight; his knuckles pale. He felt exposed, vulnerable. The weight of his earlier failures pressed down on him, and the silence amplified his doubts. Falco, ever alert, weighed their options, the burden of command a heavy load on his shoulders.

One wrong move could cost them everything—not just the lives of his men but the mission itself. He had to tread carefully, balancing Severus's impatience with the real danger lurking ahead. The enemy knew this terrain far better, and any mistake would play directly into their hands.

The trail narrowed, brambles and thorny vines lashing at their legs, trying to hold them back. The forest seemed to resist their advance, each step a struggle. After a tense hour of marching, Falco's unease grew, and he decided to halt the century. Falco raised his hand, and the column ground to a halt. The silence was absolute, unnerving. It felt like the whole forest held its breath, waiting for them to make a mistake. Falco's senses sharpened, every instinct screaming at him that they were walking into a trap. He could feel the eyes of the enemy watching them, waiting for them to stumble.

Falco's gaze flickered from shadow to shadow, branches tangled like a spider's web in front of him. He couldn't focus, couldn't hold his eyes on any one point—his heart was a trapped animal, slamming and thrashing, like it might break free if it only hit hard enough. It wasn't just noise in his chest; it was urgency, raw and desperate, clawing for a way out. A warning, clawing its way up from a place so deep it made his skin prickle and his nerves buzz. His gut twisted with that same old feeling, the one that settled like cold iron in his chest—not just unease, but something far worse. Wrong. A wrongness he couldn't name, but it pressed down on him all the same, thick and suffocating. The air around him seemed heavy, stifling, as if something hid in the dark corners. He crouched low, watching—waiting. Every second stretched thin, as if whatever it was might lash out at any moment, coiled tight, just waiting for him to make a mistake.

The scout stumbled back, breath catching in his throat, face drained of color. "They're moving," he wheezed out between gulps of air. "Different squads—coordinated." Falco's mind was a blur of possibilities and dangers. A second or two passed, and then he snapped to it, eyes locking on Varro. His voice, when he spoke, was sharp and steady. "Defensive positions," he said, barely above a whisper but sharp enough to cut through the noise. "Get ready."

He slipped down the line, relaying orders, tightening the formation, shields coming together in a practiced rhythm. This wasn't panic—this was drilled-in survival. Severus kept his eyes on Falco, his expression twisting into something caught between anger and—what? Respect? No, it couldn't be that. He opened his mouth to speak, to lash out or question, but no words came. Nothing.

A war cry split the air, followed by a storm of spears and arrows. Men

CHAPTER 3: THE SCATTERED INTELLIGENCE

crumpled, blood staining the forest floor. Germanic warriors emerged from the shadows, their faces painted, their eyes wild.

"Hold the line!" Falco roared.

"Shields up!"

The soldiers obeyed, their shields locking together to form an impenetrable barrier, the century standing as one against the onslaught. The warriors crashed against them with the ferocity of cornered wolves, their desperation echoing in every strike.

Falco was everywhere—adjusting shields, barking orders, steadying the men.

Severus froze, his sword heavy in his hand. He tried to speak, to give an order, but the words caught in his throat.

Falco took charge, directing Varro to strike back. Varro, ever reliable, rallied the men and launched a counter-attack.

Decimus fought with grim efficiency, his every move precise and deadly.
   Titus hurled his pilum, then closed in, trading bitter quips with a soldier beside him, laughing like it was all some cruel joke.

The battle raged on, a chaotic mess of a hundred men locked in a desperate struggle, the clashing steel, heavy grunts, and screams echoing through the ancient forest. Blood and sweat mingled in the thick, almost suffocating stench. Severus was shouting—he had to be—but his voice barely reached past his own ears, swallowed by the noise. Most of the men weren't even looking his way. Their eyes stayed fixed on Falco. He stood like a stone, unyielding, a beacon of strength—or maybe just stubbornness—in the chaos.

When Severus saw one of the soldiers get skewered by a spear, something in him—some tether, maybe—snapped. He yelled for a retreat, panic sharpening his voice, but the battle swallowed his command whole. Just more noise.

Falco's voice punched through the noise. "Hold the line!" he bellowed. "Stand firm!" And they did. Falco could've ordered them to face down a hurricane, and they might've tried. Varro, with that dead-eyed focus, tore into the enemy line with clean, brutal strikes. Nearby, Decimus deflected a spear and, without missing a beat, ran the attacker through. Titus? Even then, in that mess, he muttered some grim joke under his breath. Because of course he did.

The battle turned, slowly at first, then with growing certainty. The disciplined defense and calculated strikes wore down the warriors, and their rage turned to frustration.

The Germanic tribes, realizing they couldn't break through, began to retreat, fading back into the shadows. Their howls of rage turned to frustrated growls as they vanished into the thick underbrush, leaving behind a trail of broken bodies and shattered weapons. Falco held the line, watching for another attack. Silence fell, heavy and unsettling. He moved among the men, organizing the wounded and securing the line. His calmness reassured the soldiers, their fear easing as they looked to him.

Severus, hands trembling, couldn't meet anyone's eyes. He tried to swallow down his shame, but it stuck in his throat like a bitter poison.

CHAPTER 3: THE SCATTERED INTELLIGENCE

The silence stretched, broken only by the groans of the wounded and the rustle of leaves.

Falco approached Severus, his voice low and steady. "Tribune," he said, "in battle, the men need clear orders. Hesitation costs lives." "Hesitation costs lives." The words hang heavy in the air, and Severus flinched. After a long moment, he finally spoke, his voice barely above a whisper. "I won't make the same mistake again."

Falco nodded once, his expression unreadable. "We're not finished yet," he replied. "Stay focused."

The column regrouped, the forest silent but for the restless rustling of leaves. The men knew the enemy was still out there, lurking just beyond the trees. This wasn't over, not by a long shot. And as they prepared to move on, the weight of the forest seemed to close in again, and every rustle felt like a warning.

Scene 3.4: Falco's Leadership

Though the battle was over, the tension lingered, a heavy weight on the soldiers' nerves. The forest loomed, casting long shadows over the clearing. The ground was a mess of mud, blood, and broken shields.

Falco moved, weaving among the men with eyes alert and face tight. Some soldiers leaned heavily on their shields, others limped back to their spots, a few knelt, hunched over the wounded, words lost in mumbled reassurances or tight nods to steady hands trying to stop the bleeding.

Decimus moved among them, his voice calm, his presence reassuring.

Varro appeared, his face etched with exhaustion, but his eyes still sharp. He nodded at Falco: the men were in place, the perimeter secure. "Heavy losses," Varro murmured, his voice heavy.

"But the men are holding."

Falco's jaw tightened. "See to the dead," he said, voice just above a whisper. "We'll honor them later. For now, stay ready."

Varro inclined his head, moving off to relay the grim orders, while Falco's mind churned through their next steps. This ambush wasn't just a chance—the enemy had planned it, and they were still out there, watching, waiting. No time to falter.

Severus approached, his shoulders rigid, his face pale. "Centurion," he said, his voice shaking, "you overstepped your authority. Countermanding my orders—"

Men glanced up, the words hitting them like a sharp wind, eyes darting between Falco and Severus. Silence stretched, tension simmering just below the surface. Falco felt their eyes, their doubt, the sense of balance tipping dangerously.

"Your orders would have cost us all," Falco said, voice low and level, carrying just enough steel to keep control without sounding defiant. "The men come first."

Severus went pale, something cracking behind the flush of anger. He opened his mouth to respond, then stopped. He saw it in Falco's gaze—certainty, responsibility that ran deeper than titles or orders. He flinched as if struck, a mix of resentment and something like shame

CHAPTER 3: THE SCATTERED INTELLIGENCE

clouding his expression.

"You are the tribune," Falco continued, the words almost gentle, but the tone was firm. "But in the field, pride can't cloud our judgment."

Severus looked away, lips tightening into a thin line, his shoulders slumping as if he were carrying something far too heavy. Then, without a word, he turned and walked off. Just like that. The soldiers stood there, watching him leave. And there it was—a quiet shift in their expressions, barely noticeable. Respect, maybe? Falco felt it, even if they didn't say a thing.

Varro came back, voice hushed. "They're looking to you now," he said simply.

Falco didn't respond at first, eyes still on the soldiers as they steadied themselves. "We need to stay vigilant," he said finally. "The enemy's waiting for any sign of weakness."

Varro nodded, moving off again to shore up the line, and Falco turned back to the men. Exhaustion clung to their faces, the fear not fully shaken. Even discipline had its limits.

Decimus approached, voice serious. "The wounded are stable, but we're too exposed here. We need to move."

Falco nodded. "Give them a moment to regroup. Then we press on."

Titus sidled up, his usual humor weighed down by the situation. "So, boss, do we dig in and wait for the wolves, or press on and hope they're not hungry?"

Falco let a faint, dry smile twitch at his lips. "We press on. But carefully. We're not clear yet."

Titus's nod was brisk, his mockery now just a shadow in his eyes. He moved off, passing among the men with words Falco couldn't catch, but the tension seemed to ease a touch. The men began preparing to march again, movements more deliberate, their trust in Falco woven into each careful step.

On the edge of the formation, Severus stood apart, shoulders still hunched, face a mask of frustration and barely masked fear. He watched the soldiers obey Falco without question, his own authority slipping through his fingers like sand. The realization gnawed at him—his rank was an empty badge in the face of Falco's earned loyalty.

For a moment, he considered reasserting himself, but the fear of another mistake, another bloodstain on his pride, held him back. He took a breath, slow and bitter, and stepped quietly back into formation, retreating to a shadowed corner of the column.

Falco's gaze lingered on Severus for a moment, his face unreadable. He knew Severus's pride was a risk and knew the cost if it shattered beyond repair. But this wasn't the time or place to confront it—too much was at stake, and they were still in enemy territory.

The march resumed, slow and cautious, with Falco moving among the men, checking their formation, and watching the dark line of trees and the underbrush where shadows seemed to shift. Varro patrolled the flanks, silent and steady, while Decimus led the front with his gladius held low, eyes narrow and sharp. Titus, for once, kept his mouth shut, his dark humor replaced by a grim focus.

CHAPTER 3: THE SCATTERED INTELLIGENCE

Severus marched in silence, bitterness and respect, fighting a war inside him. He was starting to understand Falco's authority wasn't about orders—it was about trust and sacrifice, something Severus had only pretended to grasp. The realization was cold and unsettling, but he couldn't shake it.

The path widened slightly, branches parting as if giving way to a clearing. The soldiers' grips loosened, steps less rigid. Falco didn't relax, instincts warning him. He signaled sharply, his voice cutting through the quiet. "Hold formation. Stay sharp."

A murmur of acknowledgment rippled through the ranks, shields tightening back into place, gladii ready. They weren't out of this yet.

Scene 3.5: Regroup and Press On

The soldiers were scattered across the clearing, tending to their wounds in a near silence that felt heavy. A few low murmurs, the scrape of armor, and the occasional hiss of pain broke through the thick, damp air. Overhead, the canopy seemed to press down, swallowing what little light could find its way through. Not much sunlight, not much hope. Every breath tasted of wet earth and iron, thick and metallic. Too much blood, Falco thought, letting his eyes drift over the camp. Way too much.

He stood in the middle, watching them all, unreadable and still. The weight of their lives pressed down like the heavy sky. Varro sidled up to him, quiet as a shadow. His eyes held something that wasn't quite fear, but close enough to it.

"We lost eight," Varro muttered. "More are hurt, but most of them can still march."

Falco's face set. He nodded, barely. He couldn't let it show—this weight, this constant drag of responsibility. Couldn't afford to let them see it. "Make sure the wounded are ready to move," he said, voice steady. "We need every able man."

Varro took off without another word, the tension between them hanging unspoken. Falco shifted his focus to Decimus, who was working with that mechanical precision he was known for. Another soldier lay on the ground, his face contorted in pain. "How is he?" Falco asked, keeping his voice low. Decimus didn't look up. "He'll live," he said, his voice flat. "But I'm not sure he'll walk again." Falco winced. "Do what you can," he murmured.

He stayed there a moment longer, watching Decimus' fingers move with the care of a surgeon. The men nearby glanced over every now and then, like they were seeking some sign from their centurion—some unspoken reassurance.

Falco turned, catching sight of Titus trying—half-heartedly—to crack a joke, something about the rain letting up soon. A couple of forced chuckles followed, but it didn't lighten the air much. Not really. Severus stood off to the side, silent and stiff. He hadn't said more than a few words since the last battle. Couldn't, maybe. The weight of everything that went wrong seemed to be dragging him down, and nobody knew how to help him carry it.

Severus' back was stiff, fists clenched like he could strangle the silence itself. His eyes met Falco's across the camp—something fierce and raw flashing between them.

CHAPTER 3: THE SCATTERED INTELLIGENCE

Severus turned and strode towards them, his anger barely contained. "Centurion," he said, his voice tight, "we need to talk." Falco nodded, and Severus continued, his voice low. "I made mistakes," he said, his face hardened.

When he did, his voice was barely more than a whisper. "I made mistakes," he choked out, the words jagged and bitter. "My orders… they cost lives. I thought—" His breath caught. "I thought I knew what I was doing."

Silence hung heavy in the air. Falco could see Severus struggling, wrestling with his guilt, but didn't press him. Not yet. "Command isn't about being certain, Severus," he said finally, voice low. "It's about knowing your men and listening to them. Pride?" Falco shook his head slightly. "That gets people killed."

Severus flinched, eyes down. Falco could tell his words had hit home, and maybe that was the point—at least he hoped so.

"We've got a mission to complete," Falco continued. "The men need someone they can count on. You want their respect? You've got to earn it."

Severus nodded in a slow, deliberate motion, like he was absorbing every word. "I understand," he mumbled, barely audible, before turning and walking off. Falco watched him go for a moment, jaw tight, before shifting his focus to Varro.

Varro's face was all shadows and worry lines. "They're ready," he said, almost like he was convincing himself. "But… they're on edge."

Falco let out a breath he didn't know he was holding. "I'll handle it," he muttered, though it sounded more like he was trying to convince himself too. His eyes drifted, plans starting to form, or maybe just doubts.

He raised his voice enough to cut through the camp's uneasy murmurs. "Listen up!" The soldiers turned toward him, expectant and wary. "We've lost men today, but our mission isn't over. We still have intelligence to bring back, and we owe it to the fallen to see this through."

The camp was silent, each man listening, waiting for something to push them forward. "This isn't just for us," Falco continued. "It's for those who are counting on us to make it back. Every step we take is a victory." A flicker of defiance sparked in their eyes. Titus muttered something about dying bravely in this hellhole, and a few soldiers chuckled.

There was a flicker of something—hope, maybe—in the weary faces turned his way. Falco caught Varro's eye and gave a quick nod. "Gather everyone. We leave soon."

The soldiers, tired as they were, moved with practiced efficiency. Maybe they were running on fumes or just too used to pushing past the weariness, but for now, exhaustion seemed to loosen its grip. Falco let his gaze drift, stopping on Severus, who was making his way over. His face was tight with something unspoken, a mix of shame and a dawning realization that he needed to change, to adapt, to become a leader worthy of the men who followed him.

"Centurion," Severus said. His voice was steady, like he'd rehearsed this. "I want to help."

CHAPTER 3: THE SCATTERED INTELLIGENCE

"Help Decimus with the wounded," he said quietly. "And stay close to Varro. Watch what he does."

Severus nodded and moved off to join Decimus. As the final preparations were made, Falco signaled for the column to form up. Shields rose, weapons held steady. The forest loomed, silent and watchful.

Falco moved to the front, eyes darting down the trail. Every step forward felt heavy, like the mission's weight pressed on his shoulders, squeezing tight. Lives hung in the balance—he knew that. Every heartbeat reminded him of it.

"Forward," he ordered.

With heavy steps, the century moved forward, shields raised, their faces grim. They were battered, but not broken. They would finish what they started or die trying.

4

Chapter 4: Retrieving the Truth

Scene 4.1: The Main Scout Camp

As the afternoon of the following day wore on, and the sun began its descent once more, it felt like the forest was tightening around them. The air was heavy—damp earth, rotting leaves, and something else they couldn't quite place. Roots snaked out of the ground, tripping them up like they had a mind of their own, as if the forest was trying to keep them there. And that sense of something watching, always just out of sight, pressed on their shoulders like a hand.

The men of Falco's century moved slowly, their senses on high alert, each man a predator and prey at once. They could feel the eyes of the enemy upon them, watching their every move, waiting for them to make a mistake. No one spoke.

Falco signaled Varro to the front, and the scouts fanned out, silent and watchful, their movements practiced and efficient. Falco slipped

CHAPTER 4: RETRIEVING THE TRUTH

between the ranks, watching his men carefully. His gaze swept over their faces, searching for any sign of fear or hesitation, but he found none. Signs of life—recent, hurried—were everywhere. Footprints half-sunk into the mud, branches twisted off like something heavy had been dragged through. Varro's jaw tightened, and his gaze hardened. He saw it all.

"They're close," Varro muttered, his voice barely a breath. He pointed to a disturbed patch of earth, a smear of something darker along the dirt. "These aren't our scout's tracks. The enemy has been here recently, and they're heading towards the old camp."

Falco gave a curt nod, his eyes scanning the shadows ahead, searching for any sign of movement. They advanced, their movements slow and cautious, like wolves stalking their prey.

Severus, pale and tense, sidled closer on horseback, the fear he was trying to hide clinging to him like a shroud. His eyes darted between the shadows, searching for threats that weren't there. Or maybe they were, and that's what fear did—made you see ghosts. "Centurion," he whispered, his voice betraying a hint of fear. "How much further?"

Falco kept his eyes locked on the path, like he was trying to read something in the dirt. "Close," he said, voice calm but not quite casual. "This is where we lost contact with the scouts."

Severus swallowed hard, his grip tightening on the reins until his knuckles turned pale. He opened his mouth, closed it, then tried again. "And if the enemy's just… waiting for us?" It came out barely above a whisper, like he didn't want the words to reach beyond them. Like speaking it out loud made it too real.

Falco's eyes scanned the treeline. "Then we fight," he answered, tone flat, like the thought didn't bear dwelling on.

They continued, deeper into the green darkness, the path a treacherous maze of gnarled roots and hidden dips, the air heavy with the scent of damp earth and decaying leaves.

The silence was broken only by the rhythmic clinking of their armor and a twig snapping underfoot now and then. Each man stayed sharp; senses keyed to anything that felt off. Danger was close; they could all feel it, even if none of them saw it. Falco led the column, feeling the weight of everything pressing down on his shoulders—his men's lives, the mission, Rome itself. All of it. He tightened his grip on his gladius, the leather of the hilt rough against his palm.

The scouts, who'd been moving like wolves on a hunt, came to a sudden stop. Falco rushed ahead, senses buzzing, pulse hammering. He pushed through the thick brush and into a small clearing, where the sight made him freeze. It wasn't the abandoned camp that sent a chill down his spine—not the ripped tents or the cold, dead fire pits. No, it was the strange silence clinging to the place, thick like fog. And the glint of steel, just barely catching what was left of the day's light.

The clearing hit Falco like a punch to the gut. The weight of what he couldn't see pressed down on him, heavy and stifling. He almost felt the echoes of battles—countless ones fought on this same ground—vibrating through the silence. And somehow, it was like the Germanic warriors were still there, their presence lingering in the air, thick as mist. He stopped cold, feeling a chill run down his spine. This place—something about it was off. A place of death, really, and a brutal testament to just how cunning the enemy could be. The Romans had

CHAPTER 4: RETRIEVING THE TRUTH

been outnumbered, sure, but they were disciplined, trained for this kind of thing. They'd fought like hell, no doubt, but the enemy? They knew this ground. Used it like a weapon. And the scars—well, those stayed.

He raised his hand, fingers stiff, signaling the century to halt. Instantly, a wall of shields rose, the men forming a protective circle around Severus. "Varro, investigate," Falco commanded, eyes locked on the clearing, his voice barely a whisper.

The scout leader, along with two others, crept forward, their eyes scanning for any sign of movement, any hidden threat. Severus shifted impatiently on his horse, but Falco held him back with a look. This was no place for a Tribune, not yet.

Varro knelt, the clearing stretching out before him like a grim tapestry, his experienced eyes scanning the ground. He carefully turned over a broken shield, its leather straps rotted and its painted surface scratched and dented. He sifted through the debris, each broken piece a whisper of the battle that had raged there, his fingers tracing the cold, rusted edges of a discarded gladius. The signs were unmistakable: a desperate struggle, a swift and brutal end. Bloodstains, dark and crusted, marked the earth. Shallow graves, hastily dug and barely concealed by a scattering of leaves, offered a grim testament to the fate of the fallen scouts.

"Roman scouts," he confirmed quietly. "But... not just ours. They took documents—supplies that weren't carried by our men."

Falco's jaw tightened, but his voice was steady. "Advance," he commanded, his voice low and dangerous. "But stay vigilant. The enemy may still be near."

Severus, face pale as chalk, slid off his horse with a stiffness that made it clear he wasn't quite steady. He stumbled forward, boots crunching through broken branches and brittle, scattered leaves. The sight in front of him made him stop cold. His eyes moved slowly over the scene, taking in shattered armor, abandoned weapons, and patches of dark, crusted blood that marked the earth. His stomach churned with each detail, an uneasy roiling he couldn't shake. He hadn't seen anything like this—so much carnage. It was too much. He staggered a little, reaching out blindly until his hand found the rough bark of a nearby tree. "They... they were slaughtered," he whispered, almost like he was convincing himself it wasn't some terrible dream. Like saying it aloud might make it less true.

"Not all," Falco said, his voice grim. He kneeled beside one of the fallen scouts, turning him over gently. "Some were taken alive. Prisoners." He looked up at Severus, his gaze hard. "The enemy wanted information."

Severus seemed to shrink under the weight of it all. The blood drained from his face, and he felt almost hollow—breathless. His eyes widened as the realization settled in, slow at first, then all at once like a punch straight to the gut. Falco clapped a hand on his shoulder, meant as reassurance maybe, but it was too quick to offer much comfort.

"Varro," he called out, his voice sharp and commanding, "Gather everything of value. Maps, letters, any supplies they might have carried." He paused, scanning the clearing. "Search for signs of survivors— wounded, maybe."

The soldiers fanned out across the clearing, their eyes scanning the ground for anything of value. Decimus and Titus, their swords drawn, stood guard at the edge of the trees, their senses alert to any sign of movement in the deepening shadows. Falco moved among his men, his gaze sharp, his mind racing. He examined each scrap of parchment, each broken weapon, trying to piece together the events that had led to this massacre. The weight of responsibility pressed down on him, heavy and suffocating.

Severus approached, his face pale and drawn. "Centurion," he began, his voice trembling just enough to betray the doubt, "what do we do now?"

Falco didn't look away, holding Severus's gaze with an intensity that was almost a silent reassurance. He saw it all in the young Tribune's eyes—fear, yes, but also that creeping understanding of what war really demanded. The mess of it. The weight. "We finish the mission," Falco replied, his voice steady but not unfeeling. "We honor our dead by making sure it wasn't for nothing. And we get through this. That's our duty, Severus."

There was a moment—a heartbeat of hesitation—before Severus nodded. He swallowed hard, like the fear was something he could choke down and hide. Turning to the men, he squared his shoulders. "Continue the search," he ordered. His voice pitched a little too high at first, but he steadied it quickly. "We take everything."

The soldiers worked with renewed determination, their movements efficient and practiced. Across the clearing, Falco watched as Severus knelt beside one of the fallen scouts, brow furrowed in what looked like remorse. Maybe there was hope for the young Tribune yet. But there was still a long way to go, and Falco knew that Severus's true test was yet to come.

Varro approached, papers bundled under one arm and a torn-up map flapping in the other. "We found these," he said, voice flat. "Looks like it's got meeting points for the enemy coalition. Their leaders' spots, mostly. But..." He shook his head. "Main cache is gone—taken already."

Falco's attention drifted to a movement at the edge of his vision. Quintus stood stiff, barely old enough for battle, his youthful features etched with a mix of fear and determination. His eyes stayed locked on the fallen scouts, fear clear as day, but there was something else—determination, maybe? A promise to himself, to the ones they lost. Falco caught his eye and gave a slow nod. The kid swallowed hard, adjusting his stance, fingers firming around the hilt of his gladius. Maybe he wasn't so frozen after all.

Falco scanned the papers quickly. Names, dates, locations—scrawled in hurried, blood-stained strokes. Not a lot to go on, but enough to glimpse the depth of the Germanic tribes' resistance. Their alliances, their coordinated strategies—it was all there, just beneath the mess of ink. These tribes weren't the disorganized hordes Rome had dismissed them as. No, this was something entirely else.

The weight of responsibility settled on Falco's shoulders, heavy and unyielding. The lives of his men, the success of the mission, the fate of Rome—it all rested on his decisions. "We need to find that cache," he muttered. "Everything depends on it."

Varro nodded, grim-faced. "But if we press on, they'll know. They'll be waiting."

CHAPTER 4: RETRIEVING THE TRUTH

Falco's mind raced, weighing the risks. They were deep in enemy territory, outnumbered and exhausted. But the intelligence was too vital to abandon. He had to make a decision, and quickly.

Falco's gaze swept over the clearing one last time, taking in the carnage. The broken bodies, the scattered weapons, the blood staining the earth. He clenched his jaw, a silent vow forming in his mind. They wouldn't die in vain. "Double the scouts," he ordered, his voice sharp and resolute. "We keep formation tight. No mistakes."

Varro moved to relay the orders, disappearing into the ranks with a grim nod. Falco turned to Severus, still lingering on the edge of the clearing, face pale and hands clenched. Severus looked up, startled, like he'd been caught somewhere deep inside his own head. "Tribune," Falco called, voice steady. "We're moving. Stay close, keep the men focused."

Severus looked at him, something desperate in his eyes. Falco gave a short nod, and after a heartbeat, Severus nodded back, some of the rigidity loosening from his shoulders.

The century fell into line, their movements tense but determined. They trusted Falco, and that trust was a shield against the fear that threatened to consume them. The soldiers gathered their findings, tightening their lines. Falco watched them, feeling the same tension in his own gut. Falco took his place at the head of the column, every nerve alight.

The forest seemed to press in on all sides, the shadows deepening with each step. The rustling of leaves, the distant cries of animals—it all felt like whispers in an unseen language, a warning they couldn't quite understand.

But there was no turning back. Not now. The scouts who'd fallen, the men who followed—they had put their faith in him, and that was a weight Falco couldn't let slip from his shoulders. As long as he took breath, the mission wasn't just about survival. It was about honoring the sacrifices made and making sure they weren't in vain.

And so they moved forward, deeper into the encroaching darkness.

Scene 4.2: Securing the Intelligence

As night fell once more, it swallowed their breaths, cloaked everything in a stifling stillness. Only the soft rustle of leaves and the distant clink of armor broke the silence. Falco's century stayed poised, eyes scanning the dark thicket pressing in from all sides. The air carried an iron tang, a lingering hint of blood that sharpened their nerves. They'd found the remnants of the scout's last stand—enough to know something wicked lurked in the shadows.

Falco moved through the camp, his voice low, issuing quiet orders. He paused by a makeshift barricade, fingers tracing the deep gouges left by enemy blades. The wood was splintered, the bark almost black with dried blood. It had been a desperate fight. His tone held no hint of fear, just that controlled edge he always had. But beneath the surface, everyone felt it—the weight of something unseen watching.

In the middle of the camp, Decimus sifted through the gathered documents with a grim determination. A scattering of maps, notes, and torn letters lay at his feet, piecing together something big. He didn't have time to be shaken; methodical as always, he separated the important from the irrelevant. Varro stood nearby, barking orders to the men fortifying their positions. He moved quick, his voice clear—a

CHAPTER 4: RETRIEVING THE TRUTH

calm you could lean on when the ground beneath your feet felt like it was crumbling.

Severus lingered at the edge, his face pale, the earlier bravado slipping through his fingers like sand. Finding the bodies—the aftermath of that ambush—had hit harder than he expected. It clung to him, heavy and dark. He swallowed, tried to shake it off, but the doubt? It was there, gnawing away like some invisible creature he couldn't fight. He felt useless, like every choice he made would just drag them deeper into the jaws of whatever was out there, waiting.

Falco approached Decimus, eyeing the mess of scattered papers. "What do we have?" he asked, his voice barely louder than a breath, like he didn't want the question to carry too far.

Decimus glanced up, brow creased in that familiar furrow—half deep-in-thought, half on the edge of losing it. "Plenty of intel," he muttered, though the words came out with this rough edge, like it wasn't the good kind of plenty. Like it was a weight instead of an advantage. "The scouts confirmed the coalition's plans—tribal leaders, supply routes, meeting points. But…" He paused, almost like he was debating saying the next part. "There are gaps. It's clear the enemy took some of it."

The implications were a heavy silence between them. They had pieces, sure, but not the whole picture. It wasn't enough, not with a coalition at their throats. Falco turned, seeing Severus inching closer, face tight with uncertainty.

"We have what we came for," Falco said evenly, holding Severus's gaze. "But we're not done. This gets back to command, no matter what."

Severus hesitated, his lips parting as if to speak, but the words caught somewhere in his throat. "What if... what if they're waiting for us?" he finally managed, the question barely more than a whisper, thin and shaky.

Falco didn't waver. He glanced ahead, voice steady and low. "If they're waiting," he said, almost like he'd already rehearsed it in his head, "then we'll deal with them. Retreat isn't an option, not now."

Severus swallowed, unsure if he found that comforting or terrifying. Maybe both.

Severus's gaze fixed, but he didn't argue. Falco had no time to nurse the man's doubts; survival demanded resolve, and there was no room for uncertainty in the chain of command.

"Varro," Falco called softly, his voice cutting through the tension.

Varro was there in a flash, face hard. "Centurion?"

"Reinforce the flanks," Falco ordered. "Double patrols. Scouts need eyes everywhere."

Varro didn't hesitate. He turned, relaying orders with that same steady tone. The soldiers moved, exhaustion in their bones, but not a shred of it showed in their discipline. They knew what was at stake.

The night dragged on, the hours stretching out like an eternity, each breath making it feel even longer. Tension wrapped around them like a too-tight cloak. The soldiers waited, nerves wound tight as bowstrings. Eyes darting, ears straining—they caught every rustle, every little twitch

CHAPTER 4: RETRIEVING THE TRUTH

in the dark. Shadows shifted, or at least seemed to, just beyond their line of sight. And every moment felt like it might snap, just break.

Titus moved between the men, his usual dark humor a shade quieter. He said something to the soldier next to him, who chuckled nervously. The unease in the camp clung to them, stubborn, like the scent of blood that refused to fade.

Falco returned to Decimus. "Prioritize what's critical," he said. "If we have to move fast, I don't want to leave anything vital."

Decimus nodded, hands quick, as they sorted the mess into bundles. Severus hovered, eyes darting, mouth twitching like he wanted to speak but couldn't find the words. Falco felt the young tribune's struggle, the tightening of his fear, the constant beat of hesitation.

"Tribune," Falco said quietly, his voice firm but not harsh. "What are your orders?"

Severus looked at him, panic threatening to break through his fragile composure. He struggled to find the right words, like they were slipping through his fingers. And then, finally—barely above a whisper—"We… just get ready to leave. Carefully this time. We can't handle more losses." It wasn't exactly a rallying cry, not even close. But it was something, a beginning. Maybe even the first step toward taking charge, toward becoming whatever kind of leader he was supposed to be.

Falco nodded, holding Severus's gaze a moment longer.

"We move on my signal," he said.

A tense silence settled over the camp. The soldiers finished their preparations, their movements quick and efficient, the urgency of their task a silent hum in the air. They waited for Falco's signal, their trust in him absolute.

A twig snapped somewhere off in the distance, and Falco's eyes darted toward it instinctively. Just nerves, maybe. But then a scout stepped out from the shadows, pale-faced and tight-lipped.

"Centurion—we've got movement to the north. At least a hundred armed figures approaching from the north. The enemy's closing in."

The air hung heavy, like no one wanted to breathe. Soldiers shifted, all of them looking to Falco, waiting. Faces tense, expectant. Severus's eyes widened—panic bubbling up, and it showed.

Falco forced a calm tone, but his words came clipped. "Hold your positions," he said, scanning the line. "Get ready. Varro, reinforce the perimeter. Now."

The soldiers responded immediately, the clearing a flurry of motion as the remaining men moved with the coordination of a single being. Shields raised, blades drawn, the camp now a fortress of steel. Across the line, Falco saw the shift in their faces—doubt giving way to something harder. Falco walked the line, checking every soldier, offering a wordless nod or a brief murmur of reassurance.

Severus stood there, frozen in place, eyes locked on the dark line of trees like they might spring to life at any second. Falco approached, his voice low and careful. "Tribune," he said, "the men need your guidance."

CHAPTER 4: RETRIEVING THE TRUTH

For a second, it was like Severus hadn't heard him. He blinked, a sharp swallow following. His face lost a little color, but there was something in his eyes—a flicker of resolve. Desperation, maybe, or just the stubborn refusal to crumble. "I... understand," he said, his voice rough around the edges. Barely steady, but holding.

Falco didn't push further. It was enough that Severus hadn't shattered completely.

A soft rustling broke the silence, followed by faint, foreign voices—a harsh language that sent shivers through the Roman line. The enemy drew closer, their presence thickening the night air.

Falco felt the tension in his own gut, the familiar twist of anticipation. Falco's fingers tightened on the worn leather of his gladius, the hilt rough and reassuring beneath his touch. The first of the Germanic warriors emerged, faces painted for war, weapons gleaming in the dim light. They spread out, a line of shadows with eyes that gleamed in the dark, circling the camp. One, taller than the rest, stepped forward, lips curling into a sneer. Their leader.

"Romans," he called out in broken Latin, voice dripping with contempt. "You think you'll escape? We know what you carry. Your scrolls won't save you."

Falco's face remained unreadable. "Ignore them," he murmured to his men, his voice just loud enough. "Hold your ground."

Severus trembled, the enemy's words like a knife to his resolve. But Falco's presence anchored him and kept him from spiraling. The men stayed ready and disciplined, trusting their leader's voice above the taunts.

The Germanic warriors pressed in, testing the edges of the Roman line. Like wolves sniffing out weakness, their eyes glinted with something wild, almost eager. Falco watched them closely—saw the measured way they moved, the way they held back, calculating. They weren't charging yet, not fully, just probing the defenses, searching for the soft spots.

"Varro, Decimus—brace up here!" Falco's voice cut through the tension, sharp and commanding. He didn't shout; he didn't need to. They all felt the danger coiling tighter, ready to strike. He gestured toward the vulnerable stretch in the line, reinforcing it, hands moving faster than words.

They tightened ranks, shields pressing against each other in a solid wall, spears angled, ready. Waiting.

The camp held its breath, every man tight as a drawn bowstring. Falco could hear it all—nervous breaths coming shallow and quick, the soft clink of armor, boots scuffing the earth. His own heartbeat pounded in his ears like a drum. It was almost time.

"Steady," he said, quiet but clear. His voice was firm, a thread of steel in it. "Wait for my command."

Time seemed to hang in the air, every heartbeat heavy, the forest breathing softly around them. The leaves whispered secrets with every gust of wind, and somewhere—too close—the steady crunch of boots against underbrush marked the inevitable. A creeping fate, getting nearer. Then, before the tension could snap, Falco's voice pierced the stillness. He shouted, quick and hard—a word, more instinct than thought. It cut through everything. Silence shattered.

"Now."

Scene 4.3: Surrounded by the Enemy

The air in the camp felt like it was holding its breath, waiting for something terrible to exhale. Falco stood, feeling the tension in his own gut, the familiar twist of anticipation.

Falco's century—grizzled veterans and trembling fresh recruits alike—shifted on their feet, fingers twitching on weapon grips, eyes darting to the forest's edges.

The trees loomed dark, almost too still, the silence tense and heavy. It wasn't just the thought of the enemy lurking there, but the sense that those Germanic warriors, driven by their own sense of loyalty and blood oath to their tribes, had already closed the ring around them, slowly pulling it tight.

Falco stood in the heart of the camp, issuing orders quietly to Varro and Decimus. His face stayed calm, his voice steady, but anyone who knew him well could see the weight pulling at his eyes. That sixth sense of his—battle-honed and nearly always right—was prickling. They were being watched.

"Scouts saw movement. More than before," Varro muttered, his voice a low growl as he crouched next to Falco. "They're not just waiting—they're herding us. Testing."

Falco gave a tight nod, not needing to respond. His men, he knew, could feel it too. Soldiers had that way of sensing a storm, and the fear wasn't even trying to hide in their eyes anymore. Shields held tighter. Gladii gripped with sweaty hands. They knew what was coming; the waiting made it worse.

Severus lingered nearby, stiff and pale as old parchment. The young tribune had tried to rally the soldiers earlier, but it came out shaky, unconvincing. Falco had to step in without making it look like he was taking over, but Severus was smart enough to know. The shame sat heavy on the young man's shoulders, and Falco didn't have time to ease it off.

"Hold your positions!" Falco barked, his voice cutting through the tension like a spear. Faces turned to him, desperate for something solid to cling to. "Keep those shields high and your weapons ready. Stay together, and we hold this line."

The men straightened, nodding with grim determination, fingers tightening on their weapons. Titus, ever the one to crack dark jokes in the worst of times, muttered something about their odds, drawing a few tight chuckles. Brief as it was, the moment of humor seemed to lift the fog, if just for a second.

"Eyes on the trees!" Varro's voice followed, sharper, pulling their focus back.

Decimus approached, and from the look on his face, Falco knew the report would be grim. "Centurion," he said, keeping his voice barely above a whisper. "They've surrounded us. They're moving in slow, searching for a gap."

CHAPTER 4: RETRIEVING THE TRUTH

Falco's gaze piercing, mind racing through possibilities. They were outnumbered and penned in deep behind enemy lines. But what they carried was too valuable to let fall into the hands of those tribes—maps, intelligence that Rome needed. Retreat wasn't an option.

"Tribune," Falco said, turning to Severus, his voice even and leaving no room for indecision. "We hold this position. The Scouts will find a way. Are you with me?"

Severus's face flushed, his lips tightening like he might snap, but instead, he just nodded, swallowing down whatever anger or fear was boiling inside. "I'm with you," he said, his voice coming out strained.

Falco's nod was short, approving but curt. He had other things to worry about now. "Varro, reinforce the flanks," he ordered. "High alert. If they push, we shove them back."

Varro didn't hesitate, moving to relay the orders. The camp shifted subtly, soldiers adjusting positions, some sneaking quick looks at the trees, listening to the rustle of leaves and the haunting calls of unseen birds.

From the dark edges of the forest came a voice, harsh and grating in broken Latin. The soldiers tensed, eyes darting to where the figure emerged, broad-shouldered and marked with the war paint of a people who made this land their own. He wore Roman trophies like mockery.

"Romans," the Germanic leader called, his voice laced with mockery. "You think you can escape? We know what you carry—maps, scrolls. They won't save you."

Severus stiffened, and Falco could practically see the mix of anger and fear battling in the young man's eyes. The soldiers shifted uneasily, grips on their shields tightening. Falco didn't flinch; his gaze locked on the leader.

"Hold your positions," he said, calm but firm. They needed to hear that voice of his, unwavering.

The Germanic chieftain sneered, his voice carrying a mocking laugh. "Hide behind your shields if you like. We are many. You are few. Surrender, and perhaps there will be mercy."

Falco's grip tightened on his gladius. "Mercy?" he muttered, a cold rage burning in his eyes. He gave Varro a quick nod. A signal. Varro understood.

"On my mark," Falco murmured. "We remind them who we are."

The soldiers prepared, hearts beating faster, breaths held. The Germanic leader kept taunting, the words losing meaning, replaced by the contempt dripping from every syllable. But Falco waited; his gaze sharpened.

"Now," he said, almost a whisper.

A wave of sound crashed through the clearing—shields hitting in unison, a raw cry of defiance that seemed to rattle the trees. The Germanic warriors, clearly not expecting such a bold show, fell silent, their sneers momentarily erased.

Falco's men stood taller, shoulders squared. Severus watched, awe-

CHAPTER 4: RETRIEVING THE TRUTH

mixing with some deeper understanding. He saw, maybe for the first time, what it took to lead in moments like this.

The brief silence broke as the enemy surged, testing the Roman lines with quick, fierce strikes. Falco's voice rang out, directing Decimus and Varro, reinforcing where the pressure grew strongest. The lines held, Gladii stabbing back with cold, practiced brutality.

The clash of metal, the cries of the wounded—it all happened in a blur. Falco moved among his men, steadying them where the line wavered. Severus stayed close, eyes wide, mouth set in a hard line. He was learning more here, in this chaos, than any lesson in Rome had ever taught.

The probing attack ended almost as quickly as it began, the enemy pulling back into the shadows, regrouping. The soldiers kept their shields up, breaths ragged, knowing this was just the start.

Severus approached, his voice shaking a bit. "They... they're just feeling us out," he said, a note of realization in his tone. "This is only the beginning."

Falco nodded, his expression grim. "They're hunting for weakness," he replied, voice low. "We're not giving them one."

The forest fell back into silence, as if gathering itself. Falco ordered his men to stay vigilant, knowing that the full weight of the attack would soon hit them. His eyes met Severus's, holding there for a moment. A silent warning: Be ready.

And then it came. A roar like thunder, the battle cries crashing through the trees, and the first spear rattled against Falco's shield. The soldiers locked shields, every nerve screaming, the weight of the enemy crashing against them like a battering ram. Falco's men stood firm, ready to hold the line. Whatever it cost.

Scene 4.4: A Desperate Breakout

The assault hit like a storm without warning. War cries—guttural roars from the Germanic warriors—spilled from the treeline. Falco's century, dug in around what was left of their scout camp, braced for the chaos.

Falco held the front, shield up, eyes scanning. He'd seen this play—an overwhelming surge meant to break them, to crush resolve with sheer force. Tense breaths filled the space between the soldiers, shields gripped tight, senses sharp as knives, waiting for the first break in the trees.

"Hold the line!" Falco's voice cut the air like iron. The nods in return were small but firm, faces set hard. They all knew—they were outnumbered, surrounded. But Falco would not let this line splinter.

Then they came. Leather, fur, painted faces, eyes gleaming with a wild, murderous glint. The enemy charged, and the Roman line tightened. Shields locked. Bodies braced. The first impact was a crash, weapons hammering shields, rattling bones. Falco's orders shot out—directing Varro, Decimus, reinforcing weak points, plugging gaps. The clash swallowed everything else—steel on steel, grunts of pain, cries of the wounded.

Severus, stationed near the center, looked lost, frozen in the storm of noise and blood. Falco caught sight of him, eyes narrowing.

CHAPTER 4: RETRIEVING THE TRUTH

"Severus!" he barked. "Get in there—hold the line!" The words seemed to shake Severus back to life. He took a breath, his eyes clearing as he moved, taking his place.

A wave of doubt washed over Severus as he stumbled into position. He raised his sword, the cold steel unfamiliar in his trembling hand.

"For Rome!" he roared, charging forward with a desperate cry.

His sudden surge startled the nearby soldiers, their hesitation buying precious seconds for the Roman line to solidify.

It was unrelenting, the waves of warriors slamming into them. Falco saw it in his men's faces—every blow seemed heavier, the strain seeping into their bones. He knew the formation wouldn't hold forever. "Decimus!" he shouted. "Form a wedge—prepare for a breakout!"

Decimus gave a sharp nod, directing the soldiers with practiced efficiency. They shifted, shields moving to create a pointed edge— a risky move, but staying put was suicide. Titus moved among the soldiers, murmuring encouragements and throwing in darkly humorous jabs. The soldiers responded with grim smiles, holding onto whatever sanity his words offered.

"Ready!" Falco called. Eyes met his. Falco locked his gaze with Severus— a brief, steady nod.

"Charge!"

They drove forward, the wedge punching into the enemy, scattering their ranks. Falco led, Gladius moving with a brutal rhythm. Varro and Decimus flanked him, blocking blows and pushing hard. But the forest was thick, the terrain uneven—holding formation became impossible. Groups splintered, and the fight turned chaotic. Falco barked commands, trying to keep the men together.

Titus, ever dark-humored and defiant, anchored the rear, deflecting attacks and throwing back blows. Despite his injuries, he didn't waver, and his occasional quips won a few weary laughs from those around him.

"Keep moving!" Falco's voice was strained but unyielding. They pressed through the lines, breaths ragged, steps heavy. The Germanic warriors fought viciously, but Falco's century pushed back with the discipline of men holding onto the last thread of survival.

Near the edge of the enemy's encirclement, everything threatened to collapse. A counter-attack came—warriors rushing to close the gap. Falco's heart pounded. If the gap closed, they were dead.

"Titus!" he called, urgency sharp as a blade.

Titus turned, catching the tone, and without a word, moved to intercept. He raised his shield, gladius ready, his grin more resigned than amused now. The men hesitated, but Titus met their eyes with a bitter smile. "Always figured I'd end up here," he muttered.

He held. Alone, his shield took the full weight of the assault; every swing met with a strike of his own. Behind him, the soldiers pushed through, inching past. Falco led the charge, but his mind split—tracking every blow, every gap, every absence. When the last of his men cleared the line, Falco turned, searching.

CHAPTER 4: RETRIEVING THE TRUTH

He saw Titus alone—battered shield, blood-slicked sword, pale face set. "Titus!" Falco's voice, raw.

Titus turned, meeting Falco's eyes. There was something there— a fleeting acknowledgment, maybe even gratitude. Then, one last smile, and Titus faced the charging horde, holding his ground as they swarmed.

The century broke free, but not whole. Falco led them deeper into the forest, moving away from the main force. The clamor faded, leaving only the heavy silence of the woods.

In a small clearing, they stopped. Falco's chest heaved, exhaustion clawing at his limbs. The soldiers collapsed, their bodies trembling with fatigue. Decimus moved among them, checking wounds and securing their position.

Severus stood off to the side, eyes staring blankly at the trees, the weight of the day pressing down. He turned to Falco, voice thin. "We made it."

Falco's face hardened, grief hidden beneath discipline. "Not yet, Tribune. We've lost good men. We need to keep moving."

Severus swallowed and nodded slowly. He looked lost in it all, like he was just realizing what had happened.

Falco turned to Decimus, voice firm. "First light. We move. Prepare the men—no time to let them regroup."

Decimus nodded, issuing orders in a low, steady tone.

The soldiers obeyed, exhaustion marking every movement, but there was a sense of purpose now, a grim resolve. Each man carried the weight of their fallen comrades, a silent promise etched into their faces. Across the camp, Falco watched them, feeling the same weight in his own gut.

As dawn broke, Falco remained standing, eyes on the horizon. The light filtered through the canopy, casting long shadows over his men. He took a breath, gathering himself for what lay ahead.

The enemy was still out there, the mission unfinished. And until it was done, Falco would keep fighting—every breath a promise to the men who had fallen.

Scene 4.5: Counting the Losses

The forest felt like it was holding its breath, the morning mist clinging low, stubborn, almost spiteful. Every branch and leaf seemed to know what had been lost. Falco's century had broken free, clawing their way out of an enemy's encirclement, but no one felt like celebrating. Victory wasn't the right word.

In a narrow clearing, the men huddled in silence, faces drawn, each footfall hushed by the mulch and rot of the forest floor. They weren't talking—no need to. Falco stood, taking in the grim scene—the battered bodies of his men scattered around the clearing. Only the whispers of the leaves and their own ragged breaths filled the air, the echoes of battle fading into the distance like a bad dream half-remembered.

Falco stood in the center, turning slowly, studying each face, counting each man, and it didn't add up. Mud caked their armor, blood too—

CHAPTER 4: RETRIEVING THE TRUTH

some of it theirs, some of it not. There were murmurs here and there, soldiers checking on their injured comrades or wrapping up their dead. The silence wasn't empty; it was heavy.

Decimus came up, face tight and pale, voice barely rising above the rustle of the leaves. "We've lost too many," he said, like it was something Falco hadn't already been feeling in his bones. "And we've got a long way yet."

Falco just nodded, swallowing back whatever rose in his throat. Exhaustion? Anger? Grief? Didn't matter. "Count the men," he said quietly. "Prepare the wounded. We keep moving."

Decimus moved off, barking orders low, the men shifting like tired shadows. Over by the shallow graves, Severus stood apart, watching the earth pile on the dead. His face looked drained, eyes hollow with nights spent awake, reliving choices he couldn't take back. Varro approached him, his voice hushed like he was speaking to someone sleepwalking. "We did what we had to, Tribune," Varro said. "We had no choice."

Severus's jaw tightened, but his eyes stayed on the graves. "I should have been better," he muttered, words slipping out like he was admitting a sin. "I failed them."

Varro shook his head, not unkindly. "No time for that," he said, gesturing at the men who were still shoveling dirt over their brothers. "They need you to lead."

Severus didn't move at first, fingers curling into fists at his sides. "How do you do it?" he asked, voice barely more than a breath. "How do you carry their lives?"

Varro didn't answer right away. His gaze drifted over to where Falco was talking with Decimus, shoulders set like he was holding up a collapsing roof. "You trust in your choices," Varro said softly. "And you trust in the men beside you."

Severus's hands trembled, not sure whether to let go or hold tighter. He felt everything shifting inside, the anger and pride cracking and humility seeping in through the gaps. Leadership wasn't barking orders. It was surviving with the weight of those orders afterward.

Titus drifted between the graves, his dry, bitter humor hanging like smoke in the air. "Life's got a cruel sense of humor," he muttered to a young soldier who was still numb with shock. "You laugh at it, or it chews you up."

The boy gave a weak laugh, the kind that comes when there's nothing left but emptiness. Titus's words didn't fix anything; they just helped make the emptiness less sharp and more bearable. For a second, it was enough.

Decimus returned, face grim, as he handed Falco a blood-streaked scroll—names of the dead. Falco took it silently, eyes scanning the list, each name like a new wound reopening old ones. He closed his eyes, fighting back the rising grief that threatened to pull him under. Grief could wait.

"Falco," Decimus began, hesitant. "Some of the men—they're blaming Severus."

Falco's eyes snapped open. He turned to see a small knot of soldiers near the graves, their faces etched with anger and exhaustion. A young

CHAPTER 4: RETRIEVING THE TRUTH

recruit was speaking loud enough to carry, the bitterness spilling out of him unchecked. "It's his fault!" the recruit was shouting, his voice raw with grief. "He froze up! Didn't know what to do! And now they're dead because of him!"

Severus stood like he'd been struck, eyes wide, all that guilt clawing up to choke him. The recruit's words seemed to land like punches, every syllable cutting deeper.

"Enough!" Falco's voice cut through the noise like a blade. The soldiers fell silent, all eyes snapping to him. He stepped forward, his stare unwavering. "We're all responsible," he said, tone firm as iron. "We're all in this together."

The young soldier opened his mouth, but Falco raised a hand, quieting him. "You want to blame someone?" he continued, voice cold and steady. "Blame the enemy. Not each other."

The recruit wilted, bitterness draining out of him like spent breath. Falco turned to the rest of them, voice quieter now but still commanding. "We've lost good men," he said. "But we honor them by finishing what we started. We keep moving forward."

The soldiers nodded grimly, understanding without fully accepting. Severus hadn't moved, eyes downcast. Falco walked over, voice lower. "Leadership isn't about getting it all right," he said. "It's about pushing forward, no matter what's been lost."

Severus met Falco's gaze, something new in his eyes—acceptance, or at least the beginning of it. "I won't fail them again," he said quietly, words more like a promise to himself than anyone else.

Falco gave a curt nod. No empty words of encouragement. Just acknowledgment. Severus's road was still long, redemption a distant point, but at least he was facing the right way.

Varro appeared at Falco's side, weariness etched deep in his face. "We need to move," he said. "The enemy won't wait forever."

"Prepare to move out," Falco called, louder now. "We leave at dawn."

The men nodded, no energy for words, gathering their gear with slow, deliberate motions. The clearing felt colder, the graves stark against the earth, a reminder of what this mission was costing them.

As the first light began to creep through the canopy, Falco stood at the edge of the clearing, watching the horizon. He took a deep breath, steadying himself. The mission wasn't done, and failure wasn't an option. The men needed him, and that was reason enough.

For now, he still had breath in his lungs. And until the end, that would have to be enough.

5

Chapter 5: The Return Path

Scene 5.1: The Escape Plan

As the first light of dawn touched the clearing, the mist clung to the ground like some ghost that wouldn't let go. It curled around their ankles, almost hesitant. The forest held its breath. Birds silent, leaves barely whispering. The smell—wet earth, fresh blood, a metallic taste hanging in the air. Falco stood in the middle of the clearing, trying to ignore how his legs ached or how his shoulders felt like lead.

Exhaustion gnawed at their bones, but they pushed through it, fueled by adrenaline and the knowledge that rest could only be earned once they were safe. Every muscle screamed in protest, but their resolve held firm. They couldn't afford mistakes, not now, not with the enemy closing in.

Varro approached Falco, moving like a shadow, his face worn but eyes cutting through the haze. "They're ready," Varro murmured, his gaze sweeping over the men. "What's the plan?"

Falco's eyes moved over the men. Faces drawn and smudged with dirt and dried blood, armor dented, swords notched. Not soldiers anymore, not even men, just fragments of iron and bone held together by purpose. He let out a breath. "We move through the pass," he said quietly. No dramatics. Just the bare truth. His finger traced a thin line on the map. A trap or a salvation—no one could say yet.

"The pass is tight," Falco continued, voice low, deliberate. "But if we stay disciplined, keep the column tight, we can slip through before they realize." He was banking on that—they all were. A tightrope walk on a frayed thread.

Severus frowned, brow creasing. "What if they're waiting?" he whispered. His voice held a trace of the old arrogance, but only a trace; it was mostly doubt now, a shaky sort of uncertainty.

"They're not expecting this," Falco replied, his words steady and sharp. "They'll think we'll take the easier route. But that's not us, and that's not today."

Decimus nodded once, a stoic acknowledgment. "Scouts ahead," he suggested. "We'll use the morning mist to our advantage."

"Agreed. Varro, take the lead. Decimus, the rear," Falco ordered, looking up. No hesitation, only certainty. They couldn't afford hesitation.

Titus stood a few feet away, letting out a breathy chuckle and shaking his head. "Watching our backs again, am I?" he muttered, a thread of dark humor weaving through his words. "Can't say I'm surprised." It

CHAPTER 5: THE RETURN PATH

wasn't really a complaint, just one of those bitter jokes men make when they're toeing the edge of something worse.

A few soldiers laughed—more like a quick bark than actual laughter. But it was enough to loosen the tightness in their shoulders, just for a moment. To remind them they were still here, still breathing. For now.

Severus shifted on his feet, eyes darting around like they might find an escape in the shadows. He cleared his throat. "Falco," he began, his voice sounding rough and tight, like the words scraped their way out. "I'll... I'll follow your lead. Whatever you decide." He barely got the words out, like they left a bitter taste behind.

Falco didn't look away. He saw the fear, the shame—felt them almost, like a cold draft. And maybe Severus hated himself for it. Maybe that was what Falco saw in his eyes, underneath all the bruised pride and uncertainty. Something is trying to harden into resolve.

"We're all in this," Falco said. Just that. Nothing more. No false hope or speeches, just the plain, raw truth.

Severus nodded, swallowing hard. It was a step. A small one, but in war, sometimes small steps are everything.

"We move out at dawn," Falco told the men. "Rest if you can; gather what you need." Orders are simple, direct. No flourishes. Just like a soldier's life.

The men dispersed, slow and deliberate, checking weapons and adjusting armor. A quiet murmur among them—an acknowledgment of the dangers ahead, of what they might lose. Of what they'd already lost.

Titus moved through them, exchanging quiet words—a sardonic smile here, a sharp quip there. "This reminds me of Gaul," he muttered to a soldier nearby, loud enough for others to catch. "We were surrounded then too, but at least the Gauls didn't stink this bad." More soft laughter. A small rebellion against despair.

Varro returned to Falco, his eyes heavy with doubt. "Think we can make it through?" he asked, voice a murmur, like he didn't want the words to settle.

"We don't have a choice," Falco replied, his tone stripped down to bone. No illusions, just necessity.

Dawn bled through the trees, casting pale light through the mist. Falco signaled, and the soldiers gathered without a word. Varro moved to the front, every step cautious, eyes flicking left and right, scanning the brush. "Stay tight, stay quiet," Falco reminded them, his voice firm, almost a whisper. "Trust your training. Trust each other."

The men nodded, grips tightening on their weapons. In their eyes, exhaustion met resolve—two old friends who kept each other company.

The column started to move, each step careful, each sound swallowed by the damp ground. Severus fell into step beside Falco, his face pale, eyes shifting between Falco and the path ahead. "Thank you," Severus said, barely louder than a breath. "For not giving up on me."

Falco didn't look at him. "Leadership isn't about not making mistakes," he said quietly, words carved like a mark in stone. "It's about pushing

CHAPTER 5: THE RETURN PATH

forward. Always."

Severus seemed to take the words in; let them settle somewhere deep.

They moved deeper into the pass, the foliage thickening and the path narrowing with every step. Tension crackled in the air. Varro led them with steady precision, Decimus holding the rear, their silent glances a language of trust forged in battle. The jagged rocks above seemed to close in, the path narrowing with every step, as if the mountain itself was trying to crush them.

The pass loomed ahead, a narrow throat of rock and shadow. Falco raised a hand, the column stopping like a held breath. A sense of foreboding washed over him, a deep unease that settled in his gut. He couldn't shake the feeling that they were walking into a trap. "Varro, take the lead," he murmured. "Slow, silent."

Varro nodded sharply, his face set like stone. He slipped into the pass, and the soldiers followed, single file, each one watching the shadows, listening for the smallest hint of danger. The silence was so thick it felt alive, like it was breathing with them. Each heartbeat a hammer, each footstep a whisper.

Severus stayed close to Falco, his face tight with tension. Fear coiled tight around him, threatening to choke, but he forced it back. Trusted Falco, trusted the men around him.

One step, then another. Together, inching toward whatever waited ahead.

Scene 5.2: Through the Pass

The pass loomed up ahead, dark and narrow, like a wound cut into the mountainside. Jagged rock walls rose sharply on both sides, and thick, tangled underbrush seemed to creep inward, pressing against the path. The air hung heavy, thick with the scent of damp earth and that lingering, almost sour bite of mist clinging to their feet. The ground wasn't visible—swallowed by fog that curled up like fingers around their ankles. Every breath felt louder, every heartbeat echoed in their ears, and each cautious step forward felt like an invitation to disaster.

Varro led them, Gladius held low but poised, his eyes in constant motion, flicking between the rocky path and the dense foliage that swallowed them on both sides. Falco moved in the center, his shield ready, his gaze sweeping over his men and the narrow track ahead, weighing each decision like it could snap his men's fates in half. And maybe it could. One mistake was all it would take. He could feel the responsibility pressing down—tight in his chest, heavy in his limbs.

"Eyes sharp," Falco murmured, almost to himself. His voice barely carried, and the men, as if hearing an echo of their own thoughts, tightened their grips. No one answered; they all knew what was at stake. Somewhere, unseen, the enemy could be crouched, waiting to spring out like wolves on prey.

At the rear, Decimus glanced over his shoulder now and then, measuring the line behind him, counting shadows, tracking their silent progress. His eyes searched the rocks and the tangled bushes, fingers tracing the hilt of his sword unconsciously. Titus stayed beside him, humor dulled by the palpable tension in the air.

CHAPTER 5: THE RETURN PATH

"Not exactly the scenic route, eh?" Titus muttered, voice low and laced with a thin smile, a brave attempt to claw through the fear. But Decimus just gave him a look, a quiet one, as if to say, Not now, not here. He knew Titus's humor for what it was—a shield raised against the unease gnawing at their nerves. But there wasn't room for distraction; there wasn't room for a single false step.

The path narrowed, forcing them into single file. The air pressed in heavier, suffocating almost. The jagged rock walls seemed to lean closer, closer still, and the mist deepened, making it hard to see more than a few paces. Severus walked just behind Falco, feeling every beat of his heart drumming in his chest, loud as a war drum. His earlier resolve felt thin now, stretched tight like a bowstring ready to snap. He looked at Falco's back, steady and calm, and tried to mirror that, to take strength from it.

"I'll follow your lead, Falco," he murmured, his voice thin and barely audible.

Falco didn't turn, didn't pause. Just gave a short, sharp nod. "Stay close. Stay alert," he said, a quiet command wrapped in reassurance. Hesitation wasn't a luxury they could afford.

One of the scouts signaled a halt. The column frozen. The scout knelt, tracing faint tracks in the dirt. Falco crouched beside him, his jaw tightening. Hours old, at most. They weren't alone.

The coppery tang of blood was everywhere, clinging to the damp earth, the leaves. Falco's jaw tightened. He could feel it, feel them, eyes in the shadows, every rustle a whisper of warning. The tracks were a stark reminder of the danger lurking just beyond their sight, the ever-present threat of an unseen enemy.

Falco gestured forward with urgency tempered by caution, and Varro adjusted his pace, each step deliberate. Every noise—a rustle, a snap—sent cold adrenaline through the line. The soldiers moved like shadows through the pass, feet silent on rough stone, breaths held back as if even air could betray them.

Near the rear, Titus tried again to break the tension with a muttered joke, but it fell into the silence like a stone in water, sinking. Decimus didn't answer; his eyes were fixed forward, his jaw set.

The mist thickened, swirling around their feet. Falco halted the column. Silence, broken only by the drip of water. A scout confirmed the enemy tracks. Recent.

Tension thickened like a noose tightening. The soldiers exchanged uneasy glances, their hands gripping their weapons tighter, their knuckles white against the worn leather.

The soldiers pressed closer as the path narrowed further, shadows deepening and walls closing in. Behind Falco, Severus felt sweat sliding down his face, his heart pounding, each beat louder in his ears. They were trapped here, hemmed in by walls of stone and the tangled brush. But there was no turning back.

Varro stopped suddenly, raising his hand again. Falco moved forward cautiously, shield raised, eyes narrowing at the sight ahead—movement, just barely visible in the distance. A group of Germanic warriors. They moved in parallel, their forms blurred by the underbrush. Falco's pulse quickened, and he signaled for the column to go still—perfectly still.

CHAPTER 5: THE RETURN PATH

The enemy soldiers were cautious, scanning their surroundings. One wrong move, one noise, and everything would come crashing down. "Hold," Falco whispered, his voice barely more than a breath. He didn't dare blink. The Germanic warriors moved closer, one of them pausing, turning, eyes narrowing in their direction. He stared, suspicion pulling tight lines in his face. Seconds dragged, endless.

Falco signaled Varro and Decimus—distraction. Decimus nodded, face hardening in resolve. He picked up a small stone and tossed it into the underbrush. The warrior's head snapped toward the noise, his hand gripping his weapon. For a long moment, he stared, suspicion giving way to doubt. Slowly, he turned back, moving on with the others.

When the last sound of footsteps faded, Falco let out a breath, slow and controlled, muscles loosening. He signaled for the column to move, the soldiers following his lead with practiced precision, each step light, each breath measured.

The mist thinned as they left the pass behind and emerged into the forest. For a moment, relief—a fleeting, fragile thing. Severus looked at Falco, gratitude and humility written on his face. He didn't say anything; he didn't need to. Falco just gave a brief nod in acknowledgment. He knew the importance of what they had just survived and the thin line between success and disaster.

"Keep moving," Falco murmured. The soldiers obeyed, pale but determined. They were through the pass, but not out of danger. The enemy still lingered in the forest beyond, waiting. Falco understood that all too well. This was just the beginning. But they had made it through the first trial—alive, together—and their resolve, tempered in this fire, would be the key to whatever came next.

Scene 5.3: A Narrow Escape

The forest held its breath. Heavy mist clung to the underbrush and thick trunks like it didn't want to let go. The silence felt wrong, almost suffocating in its intensity, pressing down on Falco's century as they emerged from the narrow pass. The soldiers moved with the kind of precision that only exhaustion and discipline breed—quiet, careful, every step intentional, every breath measured. Eyes darted to every dark shadow, every swaying branch. Waiting for the inevitable.

Varro was out in front, Gladius loose in one hand, his gaze flicking quickly from tree to tree, never staying on one spot long enough to let it sink in. Falco held his position at the center, trying to juggle the terrain in front of them with the weight of the soldiers' trust hanging over his shoulders. Too many lives depended on him pushing forward, ignoring that gnawing, constant itch of danger clawing at the edges of his mind.

In the rear, Decimus and Titus watched the path they'd left behind, their expressions as hard as iron. Titus's dark jokes were buried under a layer of tension that even he couldn't shake. Not here, not now. He knew better, and Decimus didn't have to say a word—his grim stare did all the talking. Out of the pass, their protection was gone. It was all open forest now.

Falco raised a hand. The column frozen. They waited. The only sound was the distant call of a bird and the rustling of unseen things in the leaves. The silence felt alive, almost predatory. Falco strained to listen through the murk, through the growing rhythm of his own pulse that thudded like a drum.

CHAPTER 5: THE RETURN PATH

A scout approached, careful, almost reluctant. "Centurion," he whispered, his voice barely more than the ghost of breath. "Enemy patrol. Moving along a parallel path, two hundred paces away."

Falco's jaw tightened. "How many?"

"A dozen… maybe more further back," the scout replied, glancing nervously at the trees as if something might leap out at any moment.

"Inform Varro and Decimus," Falco ordered. "We're not engaging—slow and quiet withdrawal."

The scout slipped away. Falco turned to Severus, whose face was a mix of nerves and focus. "Stay close, and keep your men quiet," Falco murmured. Severus nodded sharply, understanding the weight of that command. No room for mistakes now. No time to second-guess.

They began to fall back, step by step.

Each motion measured, rehearsed, almost silent. Falco signaled in short, urgent gestures, eyes flicking over the underbrush, the shadows—anything that might hold an enemy blade or an ambush lying in wait. But it was the way the soldiers' eyes flicked back to Severus—hesitation, doubt—that made Falco's gut clench. It wasn't just the enemy they were fighting; it was the unraveling of their own command.

"Decimus," Titus's voice was barely a whisper, his usual humor replaced by a grim determination: "If we make it out of this, I'm finding a nice, quiet farm to settle down on. No more forests, no more shadows."

Decimus grunted, his eyes scanning the treeline. "Don't get ahead of yourself," he said, his voice low and steady. "We're not out of this yet."

Titus nodded, his gaze fixed on the path ahead. He knew Decimus was right. But a man could dream, couldn't he? Even in the face of death, hope was a stubborn thing.

Tension coiled tight, ready to snap at the smallest misstep. Every rustle, every crack of a twig felt like a hammer blow in the quiet.

Titus muttered something under his breath—some dark quip swallowed by the gloom. Decimus silenced him with a glare, and for once, Titus let it go. Humor wouldn't ease this tension—not this time.

Up front, Varro raised a fist. Falco felt the chill of dread run down his spine. Movement ahead. He moved forward, each step a whisper on the damp earth. He crouched beside Varro, and the optio's words came out as a breath. "There's a clearing ahead. We'll have to cross to avoid doubling back."

Falco's frown deepened. A clearing was a risk—a spotlight for anyone watching. But going back through the pass? That was worse. The enemy might already be closing in behind them.

"Send the scouts," Falco murmured, his words clipped. "We need to know it's clear."

Time stretched thin as the scouts vanished into the mist, each heartbeat feeling heavier than the last. When they returned, their faces were pale but determined. "It's clear," one scout whispered. "But we have to move now."

CHAPTER 5: THE RETURN PATH

Falco nodded sharply. "Pairs," he ordered, voice low but firm. "Varro leads. Decimus, cover the rear."

They moved across the clearing, Falco watching each group, the tension twisting tighter with every step. Beside him, Severus moved with a limp, but his eyes were focused. He crossed with Severus beside him, eyes glued to the shadows beyond. The feeling of being watched clawed at his neck, but he didn't dare turn. Distraction now was death.

Just as he reached the far edge, a rustling noise broke the stillness. His hand gripped the hilt of his gladius instinctively. Shapes emerged from the shadows, figures with eyes glinting like predators. Germanic warriors. They'd been waiting—watching.

No time. No hesitation. "Hold the line!" Falco's voice rang through the clearing, cutting through the fog of silence. The soldiers snapped into position, shields raised, eyes set. Varro and Decimus barked quick orders, their faces like stone.

Then the war cries came. The Germanic warriors charged, and the clash erupted—a brutal dance of steel and death. Falco moved on instinct, blade cutting through chaos, fighting to keep the line together. Severus was beside him; a pale mask of fear turned into hardened resolve. He fought like a man who had made peace with his purpose, at least for now.

The Roman line held, shields locking together as if the men were a single living, breathing wall. Discipline against wild fury. Falco kept shouting commands, guiding them through the storm with short, rapid gestures.

Titus, despite everything, fought like a man possessed. His humor was gone, replaced by a deadly focus, each movement precise and deliberate. He slashed, blocked, thrust—again and again, until the ground was littered with fallen bodies.

Falco's voice cut through the chaos. "Varro! We need to break through—now!"

Varro nodded, leading a charge, shields raised, pushing through with sheer force. The Germanic warriors pressed back with wild fury, but Roman discipline held firm. Slowly, their line began to crack.

"Advance!" Falco shouted, his voice hoarse. "Don't let them regroup!"

The century moved as one, shields tight, gladii flashing. The enemy stumbled, unprepared for the surge. And just like that, the Roman line broke free, emerging into another section of the forest. The fighting had stopped, but the forest still held its breath.

Falco signaled for the men to regroup. The soldiers pulled together, breathing hard, faces drawn tight with exhaustion and lingering adrenaline. They'd made it out of the pass. Barely. The enemy was still out there, somewhere in the trees, and the Roman lines were far away. But for now, they were alive. Still standing. And that had to be enough.

Scene 5.4: Approaching the Roman Lines

The forest felt alive, like it was watching them, testing them, daring them to keep moving. It tightened its grip around the soldiers, branches snagging at their armor, the morning mist thick and heavy, wrapping around their legs like chains. They kept pushing forward, exhaustion

CHAPTER 5: THE RETURN PATH

pulling at their bodies, but their minds stayed fixed on one thought: survive.

Later that day, the memory of their narrow escape from the enemy patrol—a sliver of luck in a sea of bad odds—lingered in their minds as they pressed deeper into the forest. Falco glanced around, taking in the dense woods, the shadows shifting in the wind. Every sound now felt like an omen. A bird's call, a snapping twig, the rustle of leaves that seemed too deliberate to be the wind—all of it stirred unease. They didn't want to be heroes. They wanted to stay alive. The Roman lines were supposed to be close, somewhere ahead, but the fog made everything look like a lie.

Falco pressed on, the weight of every man's fate pressing on his shoulders. His eyes darted from shadow to shadow, his ears straining for anything out of place. The brief escape they'd managed felt like a fluke, and he knew that luck had a cruel way of running out when you needed it most.

"Varro," he muttered, barely loud enough for his companion to hear over the soldiers' breathing. "Eyes sharp."

Varro didn't answer—he didn't need to. The set of his jaw, the way he moved, cautious but certain, was enough. The men followed, their shields up, gladii clenched tight. Discipline held them together, even as their strength waned. That and the whisper of safety not far beyond this endless curtain of trees.

Then came the horn, distant but clear. Marching feet, too, if you listened close. Falco's stomach dropped. They were being herded, and the Germanic tribes knew exactly where they were going. A grim realization settled over Falco. It wasn't just about the enemy's numbers anymore; they were being expertly maneuvered, their every move anticipated. He shot Varro a look that spoke volumes—a silent acknowledgment of the danger, the need for heightened vigilance. No more mistakes.

"Scout ahead," Falco ordered one of the light-footed young men, voice hushed. The scout nodded, his face pale but set with determination, before melting into the shadows. The century came to a halt at the clearing's edge, everyone crouching low in the grass, breaths held. Varro drifted among them, checking positions, his every movement a silent reminder: Be ready for anything.

Every second felt like it stretched out, like it lasted way too long. Anticipation buzzed, almost a hum in the air. Falco could hear his own blood pounding and could feel each breath rasp against the quiet of the forest. He didn't want to wait any longer—there wasn't time for it anyway. If they didn't reach the lines, the forest would swallow them whole, leaving them carved up in the shadows.

Falco threw a glance at Varro. A question, unspoken but loud enough. Varro met his eyes and gave him a firm nod—quick, steady. They both knew it; there was no time to hesitate.

"Prepare them," he whispered. Varro didn't hesitate. Orders passed quietly from man to man, and hands tightened on weapons, grips adjusting for what was likely to be a last desperate dash.

Severus was at the back, leaning hard on that makeshift staff of his. The wounds slowed him, but pride or something stronger kept him from showing it. Even now, with everything collapsing around them,

CHAPTER 5: THE RETURN PATH

he stood tall—or as tall as he could manage. Decimus gave him a nod, silent and solemn. It wasn't respect, exactly, nor pity—it was just understanding. They were all just holding on, doing what they could to keep moving forward.

The scout returned, breathing hard from his run. "Roman lines—close. But—" he swallowed, eyes flickering with unease, "the enemy's closing in fast. Not much time."

"Right." Falco took it all in. They were so damn close, he could almost picture it. Roman banners, disciplined ranks, the sigh of relief that came with it all. But not yet. The forest wasn't going to let them go without a fight.

"No stragglers," he said firmly, and the soldiers all knew what it meant. Varro moved again among the men, his voice low but steady. Titus tried to crack a joke—something about the gods and their lousy sense of humor—but nobody laughed. It wasn't the time for it.

The rustling grew louder in the distance. Falco glanced over at Severus, who met his look with a slow, steady nod. The man's wounds were bad, sure, but somehow that pain—if anything—seemed to sharpen him, like it wasn't just hurting him but waking something up inside. His features had changed—toughened maybe. It was hard to pin down, but there was new steel there.

"Stay close," Falco muttered. He wasn't just talking about proximity. They both knew that. It was about trust, about moving together without needing to spell it out. An understanding built on silence.

They moved out, Falco in the middle of the column, his senses split between the path ahead and the enemy closing in from behind. The underbrush seemed to snarl at them, tugging at their legs, forcing them to stay low and careful. The silence was heavy, punctuated by the rasp of breathing, the occasional snap of a branch underfoot, and the distant echo of pursuing footsteps—a constant reminder of the danger closing in.

Varro took point, eyes trained on the path ahead. Decimus and Titus covered the rear, gladii drawn, ready for a fight they knew was coming. Falco's eyes kept flicking back and forth, watching the men, watching the path, and straining for any hint of what lay beyond the trees. Every sound was a warning.

The century pressed on for hours, the forest seeming to grow denser with every step. The terrain became more treacherous, forcing them to slow their pace and navigate hidden gullies and treacherous slopes. Hours later, they reached another clearing, and Falco swore under his breath. He could hear the enemy now, not just hints of them—real, solid footsteps in the forest, getting closer by the heartbeat. A wave of dizziness washed over him, the edges of his vision blurring for a moment. He blinked it back, forcing his exhausted body forward. There was no time to dwell on fear or doubt, only to keep moving.

The Roman lines came into view at last, just the faintest break in the forest's dense wall. It was enough to give the men a shot of adrenaline. They pushed harder, steps quickening, hearts pounding like war drums. But Falco didn't let them rush. Not yet. Not with the enemy's shadows creeping closer.

"Steady," he murmured, the word almost a prayer. He had to keep them focused and keep their nerves in check. Severus stumbled, but before Falco could react, the young tribune righted himself, forehead furrowing in pain. Falco looked away, not because he didn't care, but because he did. Severus was fighting his own battle—everyone was.

The sounds of pursuit were louder now, pressing on their heels like hounds on a scent. Falco caught Varro's eye and gave a small nod. Varro motioned to the scouts, who drifted to the back, eyes alert, watching the shadows for any flicker of movement.

The Roman lines were so close now, Falco could almost taste the promise of safety. But the taste? It wasn't sweet like relief; it was bitter, like iron. The forest seemed ready to spit them out—ready to be rid of them—but not without taking something in return. Blood, probably. He knew that. They all knew that. A shared glance passed between Falco and Varro, an unspoken understanding of the final hurdle. The last stand before they could reach the others. And still, they pressed on, wordless and unflinching, into whatever waited past those last, shadowed steps between the trees.

Scene 5.5: The Final Assault

The century lingered at the forest's edge, the shadows and half-light creating an uneasy blur between where the woods ended and Roman lines began. In the distance, the sharp angles of the fortifications loomed, half-obscured by wisps of mist and low branches swaying in the morning breeze. Glimpses of safety—so close, like a mirage. Yet every soldier felt the weight of that distance. It was the cruelest trick the world could play: salvation within sight, danger breathing down their necks.

Falco stood, jaw clenched, eyes locked on that elusive line. Everything was screaming at him to move—move now. But instincts that had been forged in blood and steel warned him to hold back. They were on the edge, teetering between escape and disaster, and rushing now would mean collapse. He could sense it.

Without a moment's notice, the forest behind them exploded with the sounds of shattering branches and the guttural shouts of Germanic warriors, their voices echoing like the howling of wolves. The ferocity of their attack, their deep connection to the land, and their shared history of resistance against Roman expansion fueled their determination. They were closing in fast. Too fast. One last push to rip the Romans apart before they could reach safety.

"Form up!" Falco's voice cut through the panic, steady as iron. The century moved, not hesitating—every man snapping into place, shields raised and locking. The practiced rhythm of their movement a heartbeat to steady them against the rising storm. "Testudo!" Falco ordered, the shield wall rising like the hard shell of some ancient beast.

Varro moved quickly, a commanding presence even in the rush. He barked orders, adjusting shields, his eyes scanning for any signs of disorder. Decimus and Titus took their places at the rear, faces set like stone. No words needed—just the grim resolve of men who had seen too many fights like this one.

"They'll come hard," Falco muttered, almost to himself, but Varro was close enough to catch it.

"We hold," Varro answered, his voice low, eyes fixed ahead. "We didn't get this far to fail."

CHAPTER 5: THE RETURN PATH

Somewhere in the middle of the formation, Severus felt the weight of his staff, rough wood digging into his palms. He winced, the pain of his injuries shooting up his arm, but he held his grip. Pain didn't matter. Not now. He scanned the faces around him—faces that had followed him this far. Young, old, scarred, exhausted. And Severus felt, for the first time, the full burden of their lives resting on his shoulders.

The Germanic warriors burst from the mist—like wraiths, with axes and spears glinting in the early light. A roar tore from their throats, a sound driven by desperation and bloodlust. The century braced. Shields locked. Eyes narrowed.

"Hold the line!" Falco's voice didn't waver.

The enemy crashed against them with a force that shook the earth. Shields splintered under the weight, spears thrust forward, meeting flesh. The air was filled with the chaos of steel and cries—a storm of violence that swallowed everything.

Severus forced himself to step forward, despite the agony ripping through his side. His voice rang out, stronger than he felt. "Steady! Hold fast! For your brothers, your families!" His words were raw, but they resonated—a spark that cut through the fear in their eyes. A commander who showed his pain, his resolve—it was something they could follow.

Varro was everywhere at once, shouting orders and shoring up weak spots in the line. Decimus and Titus fought with ruthless efficiency, each swing calculated, each thrust deadly. Titus let out a sharp laugh as he pulled his gladius from an enemy's gut. "Bets on us making it?" he barked, and a few soldiers snorted despite themselves. It wasn't just gallows humor—it was a tether to keep them grounded amidst the carnage.

But the line wavered. The relentless force of the assault bore down on them, shields groaned under pressure, and feet slid in the mud. Falco saw it, felt it—the beginning of a break.

"Break them!" he roared, his voice rising above the chaos. He surged forward, gladius slashing through armor and bone. The soldiers followed, driven by his fury. A roar, a desperate, final attempt to push back.

For a heartbeat, it seemed enough. The Germanic front reeled. But then—a breach. A handful of warriors slipped through, eyes wild, weapons swinging. Falco's heart lurched, panic threatened to claw its way up—but he clamped down on it.

"Varro! Decimus!" Falco's shout was sharp, urgent. He threw himself at the gap, with Varro and Decimus right behind him. It was raw, close-quarter chaos—steel against skin, the wet crunch of bones breaking, the stench of blood.

Severus saw the breach, the threat of collapse, and pushed through the pain. He planted his staff and raised it like a banner. "Push forward!" he bellowed. The words rang out—not just words, but a command that demanded obedience. "For Rome!"

The century surged. A ripple of renewed strength passed through them. Severus swung his staff, catching a warrior in the temple, and the man crumpled. He barely registered the movement—it was instinct now, an extension of his will to survive.

CHAPTER 5: THE RETURN PATH

Falco's eyes caught Severus amidst the chaos, and he felt something stir—pride, admiration, maybe even hope. This was the Severus he had doubted. But not now. Not anymore.

The fight raged on—each side clawing at the edge of survival. There was no clarity, only the grinding of metal, the grunts of effort, and the rising desperation on both sides. But the century held. They had to hold. No other option.

Falco's voice reached them, steady even as the world fractured. "Stay together! We're almost there!"

The Germanic onslaught began to falter, and Falco saw their moment. He turned to Varro, his voice low but urgent. "Now or never. Get them ready."

Varro nodded with a single sharp gesture and relayed the orders. The century shifted—preparing for the final push. Severus stood beside Falco, their eyes meeting. No words needed. They moved forward, leading the charge.

Shields raised, the century struck. Desperation met desperation. The Germanic warriors, sensing the end, hurled themselves forward in a last, frenzied wave. But the Romans stood firm. They cut through the chaos, inching closer to the line that marked safety.

And then, suddenly—the Roman lines loomed into view, their comrades waiting with shields raised in welcome. A breath caught in Falco's throat—relief, disbelief. They had made it.

Falco turned to Severus, expression grave, words simple. "Well done, tribune. You earned their respect today."

Severus just nodded, exhaustion etched into his features, but beneath it—a quiet pride. They had all faced their demons, each in their own way. And for now, they had won.

As they crossed into the safety of their lines, the soldiers' shoulders sagged in collective relief. It wasn't over—not by a long shot. The road ahead was dark and uncertain. But for now, they breathed. They had survived the storm.

And sometimes, that was victory enough.

6

Chapter 6: The Price of Duty

Scene 6.1: The Enemy's Final Push

As the sun climbed its way into the sky, the clearing loomed ahead—open ground, treacherous in its simplicity, just a stretch between Falco's century and the safety of the Roman fortifications. It was close to midday, and the sun, a burning eye in the sky, beat down mercilessly on the soldiers, their armor heavy with the weight of exhaustion and fear. Not that it felt like safety. No illusions of relief or sanctuary lingered in the eyes of his men. Not with those war horns. The Germanic war horns howled once more, their echoes threading through the forest like a predator's warning, a call to arms that echoed the deep-seated resentment against Roman encroachment, the tribes' shared history of resistance fueling their final stand. It was a sound that spoke of desperation, of a final, all-or-nothing gamble, fueled by the fierce pride and unwavering loyalty that bound the Germanic tribes together, their shared heritage and deep connection to the land driving their last stand against the Roman invaders. Ahead, Falco saw the clearing—a flat stretch of ground leading to the Roman fortifications.

"Form a defensive line here!" Falco's voice rang out, steady, sharper than his heartbeat thrumming in his ears. "Varro, position the men!"

They moved without hesitation, as if instinct drove their limbs rather than thought. Shields up, Gladii ready. The march had drained them, leaving dark hollows beneath eyes that still flickered with determination. A battered wall, but unyielding. And Falco felt it—not just their fatigue, but something else—something like a thread pulling them together, a silent resolve in each strained face. Severus could almost touch the unspoken resolve binding the soldiers together—something born of shared pain and purpose. It was a unity he hadn't known existed, a bond forged in the heat of every bad decision and every drop of blood spilled.

Severus limped forward, leaning on a makeshift staff, each step a testament to his stubborn will. "What's the plan?" Severus muttered. Falco didn't flinch. "We hold," he answered. Nothing more to say. He looked to Decimus. "Ready the men for a counter," he called out. Decimus nodded, his eyes betraying no doubt.

Varro barked quiet orders, and the century tightened ranks. The earth shifted underfoot—a grim reminder that the approaching enemy was no figment of his weary mind. They were coming. They were close.

Across the line, Severus stepped forward, and for a moment, Falco thought he might object again. But the tribune surprised him. "Men of Rome!" Severus's voice broke through the tense silence, strained and rough but clear. Falco watched the soldiers' faces as Severus spoke, seeing the way they straightened, the doubt giving way to something

CHAPTER 6: THE PRICE OF DUTY

like hope. A small shift, but a shift nonetheless. "You've bled together!"

"Now, hold this line—for each other, for Rome!"

His words fell heavy, sinking into each soldier like iron being forged. A faint murmur traveled through the ranks, barely audible over the mounting storm of sound from the treeline.

The Germanic warriors burst forth, shadows solidifying into a wave of snarling fury. They charged with cries that cut through the air, with weapons and iron and a desperation Falco knew too well. The Romans braced.

"Hold!" Falco shouted, his arm rising like a dam against the tide.

The initial clash reverberated like a battering ram, shaking shields and rattling teeth as the century absorbed the blow. But the century held. Spears shot forward, thrust after thrust, meeting the wave with a steady, relentless rhythm. The line held, straining like an old oak against a relentless wind but refusing to give way.

"Steady!" Falco's orders rose over the din of steel and the groans of the injured. He pushed through the ranks, his gladius ready, shouting orders, steadying hands that trembled, filling gaps where men had fallen. "Shields up! Forward—just a step!"

In the center, Severus fought with a stubborn ferocity, each swing of his staff knocking the legs out from beneath oncoming warriors. His eyes were wild with pain, but something else glimmered there too—defiance. His presence bolstered those around him; a wounded man holding the line seemed to shame others into finding their strength.

Varro moved like a practiced hand, sealing breaks before they became gaping wounds, reinforcing the line with sharp commands and swift strikes. Titus, fighting beside Decimus, managed a grim chuckle between parries, "Persistent bastards, aren't they?"

Falco's eyes darted across the line. The enemy pressed harder, their resolve like a hammer pounding against the Romans' shields. He could see the exhaustion in his men's eyes, the way their shields bent beneath the blows. If this held, they wouldn't last long—not alone.

"Severus!" Falco called out, his voice nearly breaking. "Signal for reinforcements!"

Severus met his stare, understanding in his eyes. He raised his staff, waving it with what little strength remained, in a desperate attempt to reach the fortifications. Falco had no choice now—just to hope.

The enemy's cries surged, frenzied and wild. A group of Germanic warriors broke through, and Falco didn't hesitate. "Decimus, Varro—reinforce!" They moved swiftly, dispatching the intruders with ruthless efficiency. The line reformed, tighter, more desperate, but intact.

Then, a sound cut through the chaos—a sharp, clear horn from the Roman lines. Hope. It was something tangible now, something they could grab onto.

"Reinforcements!" Severus's shout came as both a command and a prayer. "Hold the line! Help is coming!"

The enemy, though, seemed beyond reason, their resolve solidifying into something unbreakable. With a furious cry, the enemy gathered for

CHAPTER 6: THE PRICE OF DUTY

a final, desperate push across the blood-soaked clearing. The Romans braced.

"Ready!" Falco's voice strained with the weight of it all. "Hold the line!"

The wave hit. Shields and spears clashed in a brutal dance, weapons flashing and feet slipping on blood-slicked ground. Each clash jarred bone and bruised flesh, every heartbeat an ongoing battle against fatigue and agony. Falco moved through it all, each swing of his Gladius precise, instinct guiding his arm while fatigue threatened to drown him.

Severus held his ground, refusing to let pain weaken his resolve. Varro and Decimus, unwavering, cut through the chaos with practiced grace, their faces set in the grim mask of experience. But the line was failing, fraying at the edges, men dropping to their knees under the relentless assault.

Then, the reinforcements arrived—a surge of fresh soldiers charging into the fray, shields up, gladii ready. The enemy hesitated, surprised by the sudden surge of Roman reinforcements, their eyes widening in fear at the unexpected onslaught.

"Push forward!" Severus's voice rose, cracking with the strain. "Drive them back!"

The Romans pressed, their Gladii cutting through the disarrayed enemy. The Germanic warriors faltered, then broke, fleeing the field in a panicked retreat. Cheers erupted among the century, voices rising above the clamor as the enemy scattered.

Falco lowered his gladius, his limbs heavy with exhaustion. He turned to

Severus, their eyes meeting, the weight of the moment passing between them in silence. "We held," Falco murmured, more to himself than anyone else.

Severus nodded, the exhaustion in his face softened by a quiet pride. "We held," he echoed.

The soldiers regrouped, their breaths heaving, bodies battered but standing. Falco stood among them, feeling the exhaustion in his own bones. They had survived and won a moment of respite in a place where none had seemed possible. But Falco knew it wasn't over. Not yet. Ahead lay new dangers, more battles, and the critical mission still unfinished. But for now, the line had held. For now, they had earned this fleeting breath before the storm resumed.

Scene 6.2: Holding the Line

The clearing was a broken, blood-soaked mess of bodies and chaos. Falco stood, taking in the aftermath of the battle, the cries of the wounded echoing around him. Romans and Germanic warriors lay twisted where they'd fallen, limbs tangled with shields and shattered weapons. The ground was a churned mix of mud and spilled blood, like the forest itself had swallowed both the dead and dying.

The air stank of sweat and iron, a sharp bitterness that clung to the back of the throat. The silence was broken only by the ragged breathing of the wounded and the distant calls of crows, drawn by the scent of death.

In the lull, every noise seemed amplified—labored breathing, the groans of the wounded, the distant rustle of the enemy regrouping for another

CHAPTER 6: THE PRICE OF DUTY

attack. It was the kind of stillness that felt heavy, like it might crush you if you let your mind linger too long.

Falco moved through the ranks, the dirt and blood weighing his armor down, but his voice stayed clear, cutting through the murmur. "Hold the line!" he shouted, firm and relentless, as if shouting it louder would anchor them all to the earth. He had to keep them focused, even when everything in him screamed to sit down and catch his breath. But Falco couldn't afford to listen to that voice, not now. His armor felt like a second skin, stained and battered, but he didn't notice the weight anymore. The leather straps dug into his shoulders, the iron plates heavy against his chest, but all he felt was the weight of responsibility, the lives of his men hanging in the balance. Just the eyes of his soldiers looking to him for strength he wasn't sure he had left to give.

Varro and Decimus reinforced the shield wall, their quiet orders snapping the men back to the task. It was instinct for them by now—a rhythm drilled into their bones over years of blood and dust. Varro's expression was cold, calculating, like a man watching storm clouds gather. Decimus, always the silent one, gave Falco a short nod. Nothing more needed to be said. They all felt it—the crackle of something about to shatter.

Nearby, Titus muttered a joke to one of the archers, something bleak but meant to break the tension. The archer chuckled weakly, but his fingers still twitched nervously on the string. Titus's humor had always been a grim lifeline, a reminder that as long as you could laugh, you weren't dead yet. Not quite.

Falco straightened, feeling the eyes on him, knowing they were looking to him for more than orders. They needed purpose, a reason to still be standing when their legs were screaming to run. "We are Romans," he said, steadying his breath. "We hold the line—for each other and for Rome."

The words were worn, familiar, but they seemed to light something in the men—a defiance, a stubbornness to stay on their feet a little longer. Backs straightened. Shields tightened. Gladii gripped like lifelines.

Then came the sound. The low, rolling rumble of the enemy's horns from deep in the forest. An awful, distant thunder. Falco's face set. They were coming again, and this time it felt like they were bringing the entire damn forest with them. The Germanic warriors poured out from the treeline. "Archers, ready!" Varro barked. The archers didn't hesitate, arrows drawn and eyes narrowing, focusing only on the distance between them and the advancing horde. Varro's signal dropped like a blade, and arrows cut the air with a deadly whisper, finding their marks among the charging warriors. Some fell, but not enough. Never enough.

Falco planted himself where the pressure was worst, the center of the line. He could feel the earth trembling beneath the pounding of their feet. He shouted, "Steady!" but it was more of a growl, an order as much to himself as to the soldiers.

The enemy hit them like a hammer. Axes and swords crashed against the Roman shields, and the impact ran through their bones. The shield wall shuddered but held, spears darting through gaps like lightning to find flesh. Beside him, Severus—who had once seemed so out of place with that damn staff—now wielded it like a blade. He fought without hesitation, using the staff to deflect strikes to trip men in the midst of their charge. It wasn't just desperation; it was skill; it was purpose.

CHAPTER 6: THE PRICE OF DUTY

"Hold the line!" Severus called, voice breaking but still commanding. "We're not giving an inch!"

And they didn't. They held, each man bracing himself against the weight of the assault. The exhaustion in their eyes didn't vanish, but it hardened into something else. A refusal to let go of their brothers beside them.

Falco saw the line starting to thin and felt the desperate weight of time slipping away. He scanned for something, anything, to buy them another moment, and then the idea hit like a cold slap. "Varro!" he called out, urgency pushing his voice higher. "We need to fall back to higher ground!"

Varro didn't argue, didn't hesitate. He moved with the practiced speed of someone who understood what was at stake. The command rippled through the ranks, and the men began to shift, retreating in unison towards the small rise behind them. It was barely an incline, but it was enough to force the enemy to come uphill. Enough to make them bleed for every step.

"Stay together!" Falco urged, voice-breaking but unyielding. "Move as one!"

They reformed on higher ground, backs to the fortifications. Archers repositioned to the flanks, their bows ready in case the line broke. Falco glanced towards the forest; the enemy was closing the distance fast. Too fast.

The charge came, a thunderous wave crashing against the shield wall, and for a moment, all was chaos. The earth had turned to slippery mire, and the shields quivered beneath the relentless battering of enemy blows. But the line held—barely. Blood splattered the air, mixing with the rain of dirt and sweat. Somewhere in the mess, Severus fought on, relentless. Falco caught a glimpse of his face, eyes blazing with a strange, almost reckless determination. He'd found something to fight for.

"Keep pushing!" Severus shouted, his voice carrying a weight that made men move even when they had nothing left.

Falco felt it too. A quiet pride swelling up, seeing Severus grow into the leader the men needed him to be. But there was no time to dwell on it. The line was breaking, exhaustion digging its claws into every man there. Just when the weight felt unbearable, the Roman horn sounded from the fortifications. Reinforcements.

The signal rang clear through the chaos, lifting the fog from the soldiers' eyes. Hope. It was something tangible now, something they could grab onto. The enemy, sensing it too, rushed forward with renewed madness.

"Hold on!" Severus's voice rang out, more a command than a plea. "Help is coming!"

Then, like the tide turning, the reinforcements crashed into the enemy's flanks. Caught off guard, the Germanic warriors faltered. That hesitation was all the Romans needed.

"Push forward!" Severus roared, voice like iron. "Drive them back!"

The soldiers surged, shields bashing forward, gladii striking with grim resolve. It wasn't clean or pretty, but it didn't have to be. The enemy broke, stumbling back into the forest, their roars turning to panicked cries. The Romans let out a ragged cheer, watching their foes scatter into the trees.

When the dust settled, Falco felt a wave of exhaustion crash over him, almost knocking him off his feet. He turned to Severus, eyes meeting with a silent understanding. "Well done," he muttered, his voice rough and tired.

Severus only nodded, his face pale but full of something deeper than relief. Pride, maybe. They had held the line, and for now, that was enough.

Scene 6.3: Severus's Redemption

The enemy pressed down with all their might, a desperate wave of bodies and blades crashing against the Roman line. Outnumbered and weary, the Romans fought back with the ferocity of cornered wolves, their gladii flashing, their shields a wall of iron against the onslaught. But the enemy's numbers were overwhelming, their attacks relentless, and the Roman line began to buckle under the strain.

The line of Roman shields shuddered under the Germanic onslaught, their savage cries ripping through the chaos, heavy with fury. The soldiers dug their heels in, shields up and muscles screaming with each fresh impact. The air was thick with the stench of sweat and blood, the ground slick with mud and gore. They couldn't let go. Couldn't even think about it. They just had to hold.

Severus stood there, dead center in the chaos, each breath a struggle, coming in ragged and shallow. His wounds ached, sure, but they were a distant thing, somewhere buried under the weight he carried—something heavier than iron. He saw the exhaustion in the eyes around him, the men's hands trembling as they clenched their gladii tighter, the formation wavering like a fraying thread.

Falco's voice cut through the roar, sharp and strong. "Hold the line!" The command rang out. "Reinforce the center!" There was no hesitation—just obedience, pure instinct. The men shifted and closed ranks. But Severus knew it wasn't enough. The blows kept raining down, and the line felt like it might crumble at any moment.

Leadership wasn't about bravery—it was about the crushing weight of responsibility. These men were looking to him now, their survival pinned to whatever he did next.

"Severus!" Falco's shout reached him, barely breaking through the noise. "We hold this position!"

Severus turned, met Falco's stare—an unspoken test, a torch passed. Everything Falco had taught him—all the drills, the discipline, the moments of doubt. Now, it was up to Severus to carry that weight forward. The look wasn't angry or anxious. It was steady, unblinking, daring him to rise or be crushed.

Deep breath. He shut out the doubt, shoved down the pain clawing at his ribs. He had failed before and stumbled in places he should have stood strong. Not this time. He wouldn't run, wouldn't shrink from what needed doing.

"Men of Rome!" Severus called, voice rough but solid enough to cut through the cacophony. "I know you're hurting! I know you're tired!

CHAPTER 6: THE PRICE OF DUTY

But we're Romans. We do not break!"

Eyes turned toward him—tired eyes, bloodied faces—searching, desperate for something to cling to. Severus felt the knot in his chest tighten, but he didn't stop.

"We've come too far to fall now," he shouted. "Hold for your brothers! Hold on for those who fell beside us! Hold for Rome!"

Resolve flickered, took hold, and grew into something harder. Shoulders squared, Gladii gripped with white-knuckled certainty. The words weren't magic, but in their grim silence, he saw it—they still believed in something. They'd follow him if he led them.

"Form up!" Severus barked, his voice firm, almost steady. "Reinforce the line! We hold, no matter what comes!"

Varro rushed to pass on orders, quick and sure. Decimus and Titus moved to the flanks, their faces pale but set like stone. The line shifted, shields raised, ready to take the next blow.

The enemy surged forward, roaring louder, their ferocity almost tangible. Severus could feel the ground tremble with their charge. But he held his place, shouting over the din, "Steady! Hold your ground!"

The clash came like thunder—shields rattling, weapons slamming, bodies colliding. The force of the assault was brutal, and Severus felt it reverberate through every bone, but he dug in and gritted his teeth. The soldiers around him mirrored his defiance, their shields absorbing the impact like a wall of iron.

"Push back!" Severus shouted, voice ragged. "Drive them off!"

The soldiers responded, thrusting forward in unison, a single movement honed from years of harsh training. The front ranks of the enemy staggered, cries of pain swallowed by the roar. Still, more came. More always came.

Severus waded into the thick of it, staff swinging low and fast, striking at legs, disrupting the momentum. It was instinctual, almost mindless—the need to keep fighting, to keep moving. He didn't have time to register the pain, the exhaustion, the sheer terror gnawing at the edges of his mind.

Falco caught sight of Severus's defiance, something shifting in his eyes. The doubt he'd carried—maybe still carried—cracked just a little. He saw something in Severus now, something more than the Tribune he'd trained.

"Reinforce the center!" Falco called out, his voice a lifeline in the chaos, pulling stragglers back into formation. Still holding steady, still strong.

The enemy's numbers seemed endless. They threw themselves against the line, relentless, relentless. The Romans held, shields interlocked, each man's life bound to the next. Severus's presence wasn't just a figurehead—it was a reminder that, if he could stand there among them, then so could they.

He saw an opening in the chaos. "Archers!" he bellowed, signaling a barrage. Arrows flew, striking down enemy leaders with precision honed from countless skirmishes. A momentary pause in the onslaught—the enemy hesitated, leaders fallen, confusion spreading.

CHAPTER 6: THE PRICE OF DUTY

"Advance!" Severus shouted, urgency flooding his words. "Push them back!"

The soldiers moved as one, shields raised, swords driving forward. The Germanic line wavered, caught off guard by the sudden counterattack. Severus felt a brief, exhilarating surge—hope where there had been only fear.

But it wasn't over yet. The enemy rallied; their rage redoubled. Severus knew this was it—the final push, the moment where everything would either hold or shatter completely.

"Hold together!" Severus yelled, his voice hoarse. "We're almost through this!"

The soldiers locked eyes with the enemy, shields bracing once more. Every muscle in Severus's body screamed in protest, but he refused to listen. No room for pain. No room for doubt. Just hold.

The clash came again, more vicious, more desperate. The noise was deafening, the cries of battle drowning out all other thought. Severus fought like a man possessed, the staff an extension of his will, striking out wherever he saw weakness. He caught glimpses of the others—Varro, Decimus, and Titus—each of them giving all they had, fighting for more than just survival.

And then, just when it seemed like they'd break—the enemy faltered. A ripple of hesitation and exhaustion, and then the retreat began, a slow unraveling of the relentless assault. A cheer rose among the soldiers, ragged and hoarse, the relief almost crushing in its intensity.

Severus lowered his staff, slumped back, breath coming in shallow, painful bursts. He turned to Falco and caught the look of respect in the centurion's eyes—a shared understanding. "We held," Severus said, voice barely a whisper but heavy with something deeper. Pride. Exhaustion. Relief.

Falco nodded, his voice thick with unspoken gratitude. "You did well, Severus."

The soldiers regrouped, bruised and bloodied but alive. Ahead lay more trials, more battles. But for now—for just a moment—they'd earned a brief, precious pause.

Scene 6.4: Race to Safety

The canopy was behind them now. Falco's century spilled out from the forest, the shadows of the trees fading into a narrow stretch of open ground. Just a few hundred paces to the Roman walls, but it might as well have been miles. Dark clouds rolled above, heavy with unshed rain, mirroring the weight in the men's hearts as they stood exposed. Falco's fingers twitched, and he forced them to still as he raised a hand to halt the century.

There they were—the walls. Stone and timber, looming in the distance. Safety. Yet between here and there stretched a patch of death waiting to happen, if the enemy picked this moment to appear. Falco scanned the distance, each heartbeat loud in his ears. Nothing moved. Not yet.

"Hold," he said, voice low but sharp. His men shifted into formation, shields coming up, gladii raised, their exhaustion hidden beneath layers of instinct and training.

CHAPTER 6: THE PRICE OF DUTY

Severus stood nearby, breathing shallow, his face drawn tight. Blood stained his side, the cloth beneath the armor darker than it should be. The tribune had fought through every ounce of pain to get them here, and it showed. But even now, with every inch of him crying out for rest, Severus stayed upright, his fingers white-knuckled around the hilt of his gladius.

Falco met Severus's eyes. A fleeting moment. No words. Just the recognition of what they'd endured, the unspoken agreement that neither would let this fall apart now. Severus gave a brief nod, a silent assurance that he wasn't done yet.

"Stay close, no stragglers," Falco ordered. He could hear Varro repeating the command in that clipped, steady tone of his, words rolling down the line. Decimus took the point, planting himself like a damn statue at the head, a quiet force holding them together. Somewhere in the middle, Titus muttered to the men nearby, his voice almost cheerful despite the weight of it all.

"Just a quick sprint. With death breathing right behind us," Titus grumbled, and the men gave tired, humorless chuckles. A laugh in the face of terror—that's how they coped.

In the silence that followed, a distant horn cut through the air, and Falco's gut twisted. No mistaking that sound. The Germans were coming. He turned his head, listening for the drumming feet in the distance. The hounds had caught their scent.

"We move," Falco said, louder this time, urgency threading through his words. "Shields high!"

The century pushed forward, boots sinking into soft ground with every step, their eyes flicking between the walls ahead and the forest they'd left behind. Falco could almost feel the tension humming through their ranks, a living thing crawling up their spines.

Severus was limping, though he tried to hide it. Stubborn. Always too stubborn. He kept pace, jaw clenched, eyes forward. Falco kept a close watch, ready to step in if the tribune faltered. But pride kept Severus upright.

The walls were growing larger now, shapes moving atop them—Roman soldiers readying the defenses. The horn must've reached them. They were expected. That should have been reassuring, but Falco could hear the pounding feet behind them now, the shouts, the cries growing louder.

"Double time!" Falco roared, the command rolling down the line. They broke into a jog, weariness momentarily set aside as the urgency of the moment washed over them. Their strides fell in sync, even the wounded matching the pace; the fear of what followed spurred them on.

The distance felt endless, a stretch of ground that seemed to grow longer with every step. Don't look back, Falco told himself. Don't dare look back. He kept his eyes on the walls, the gates, and the Romans moving with frantic efficiency above.

Then, the whistle of arrows cut the air. The first volley arched overhead, iron heads glinting briefly before they fell upon the advancing enemy. A chorus of shouts and cries erupted behind them. Some of the Germans stumbled, struck down by the Roman archers. The soldiers on the walls

CHAPTER 6: THE PRICE OF DUTY

cheered, voices mingling with the noise of steel and agony below.

Falco glanced at Severus and saw the pain etched deep into his features. "Almost there," he murmured, barely a breath between them. "Just a little more."

Severus didn't speak, just tightened his grip and kept moving. A step at a time, fighting for every inch.

They reached the base of the walls, and the gates groaned as they began to open. Shouts from above, urging them on. The enemy was close now, the roaring right on their heels. Falco could almost feel their breath on the back of his neck.

"Through the gates!" he bellowed, and the soldiers surged forward. Severus stumbled, the wound catching up with him, and Falco grabbed his arm, hauling him upright. Together they staggered into the gate, the others streaming in behind them.

The gates slammed shut with a deafening clang, the bar sliding into place as the first of the Germans reached it. Their roars turned from triumph to fury, weapons striking uselessly against iron and wood. Falco's chest heaved, his breath coming in ragged bursts as he took in the scene—the men leaning against the walls, trying to catch their breath, faces streaked with mud and blood. They were alive. Barely.

Severus lowered his sword, shoulders slumping under the weight of exhaustion and relief. "We did it," he breathed, his voice thick with something like disbelief.

Falco turned to him, the adrenaline slowly ebbing away. He placed a hand on Severus's shoulder, a firm grasp. "You held them together," he said, words simple but heavy. "You led when it mattered."

Severus blinked, as if the praise were a foreign thing. But he gave a quick nod, swallowing whatever response might have come.

Around them, the soldiers were regrouping, straightening up despite bruised ribs and aching muscles. The enemy still battered the gates, but the sounds were muffled now, the walls standing firm. They had survived another day. For a moment, that was all that mattered.

Falco knew it wasn't over. It never was. There'd be more battles, more losses, and more choices to face. But for now, they had made it back. And sometimes, that was all you could ask for.

Scene 6.5: Reflecting on the cost

By midday, the Roman fortifications seemed to breathe in shallow, strained breaths, like a wounded animal nursing its pain. Falco stood, leaning against the stone wall, taking in the aftermath of the battle. Broken murmurs of soldiers drifted like ghostly whispers; the occasional clank of armor sounded hollow. The place reeked—of blood, sweat, and earth churned into mud. Falco could taste it on his tongue— bitter and metallic. The silence held its own weight, oppressive, like fog clinging to the ground. Safety, if you could call it that, felt thin and brittle, cracked by the absences that hollowed out the ranks. Faces Falco knew like his own were gone. And every missing face was a new scar, an ache settling deep into his bones.

He stood apart from the men, eyes locked on the shadowed forest beyond the fort. The ground felt solid beneath his feet—a strange

CHAPTER 6: THE PRICE OF DUTY

sensation after so much running, dodging, and striking. Each step, each breath in that cursed forest had been a gamble, and now, here he was. Safe. Yet something in him refused to let go, still coiled, waiting for an attack that wasn't coming.

Severus approached, moving slowly, steps uneven. Someone had patched him up, but he looked half-ghost. He stopped a few paces from Falco, hesitating, like a man testing the thin ice of a frozen lake. But the silence between them wasn't empty—it held the weight of what they'd survived.

"You did well out there, Tribune," Falco said, voice low, steady. There wasn't any praise, just the blunt recognition of a truth they both knew.

Severus exhaled slowly, like letting go of a breath he'd been holding for hours. "I made mistakes," he muttered, the words barely escaping his lips. "Men died for them."

Falco turned to look at him, eyes unblinking, hard. "We all made mistakes," he said. His voice was rough, with the edge of battles survived. "But you didn't quit. You stayed with your men when things turned bad. Earned their respect. Not everyone can do that."

Severus clenched his jaw, the muscles twitching. Falco knew that look, knew how losses carved themselves deep, how guilt settled into a man's soul like poison. But there was something else too—something Severus hadn't had before. A hardness. A resolve.

"I've learned a lot from this mission," Severus said, words coming firmer now. "About leading... and about myself."

Falco nodded, seeing the reflection of his own struggles in the young officer. Command wasn't just orders and victories; it was facing your own failures and finding the strength to rise again. He knew what it felt like to stumble through that darkness.

"There's always more to learn," Falco said, almost to himself. "But you've started. That's what matters."

The younger man dipped his head, a silent acknowledgment. But Falco could see it—there was something still caught in Severus's mind, something unresolved. Severus shifted, uneasy, and then finally asked, "The intelligence we brought back—do you think it'll be enough?"

Falco let the question hang, eyes drifting back to the forest, the edges of the trees lit by the dim torches. "It's a start," he said, voice thoughtful. "A warning. But what happens next—that's where it'll be decided."

A moment passed as the truth of those words sank in. It wasn't just about what they'd done; it was about what came after, about the decisions that lay ahead. A mission wasn't an ending—it was just another beginning.

Varro's voice cut into the quiet, drawing Falco's attention. "Centurion, the men are gathering for the fallen," Varro said softly. "They're waiting for you."

Falco gave a brief nod. He glanced at Severus, eyes questioning. Severus hesitated, but only for a moment. Then he followed, the two of them walking in step behind Varro towards the center of the camp.

The soldiers stood in a loose circle, eyes weary, faces grim. Decimus

CHAPTER 6: THE PRICE OF DUTY

was at the front, holding a torch. His face, always stern, seemed older, weighed down by grief. The small flame in his hand flickered, shadows dancing over the silent crowd. Falco and Severus took their places at the head, and Decimus stepped forward.

"We lost good men today," Decimus said, voice steady, though his grief seeped through. "Men who fought beside us, who bled with us, who died for Rome."

A murmur ran through the ranks, heads bowed in agreement. Titus, still favoring his wounded shoulder, muttered something dark and dry. A few soldiers managed weary smiles—a thin crack in the heavy grief. Somehow, even in their mourning, a flicker of humor kept them grounded. It was all they had left sometimes.

Decimus spoke again, voice firm with something almost reverent. "We honor them by standing strong, by holding to the bonds we've forged through this ordeal. They live on, so long as we remember their courage."

Silence followed, heavy as lead. Each soldier bowed his head, and in the stillness, Falco felt the closeness of the men around him. They weren't just soldiers—they were brothers. And that bond was forged in blood and tested in darkness. It was a bond he was willing to bear, no matter the cost.

When Decimus stepped back, Falco took his place at the front. He looked at each face—etched with pain, exhaustion, and something else. Something unbroken. "You've done Rome proud," Falco said, voice rough but sincere. "And I'm honored to have led you. We lost brothers today, but their memory will drive us to stand strong—for them and for each other."

The soldiers met his gaze, their nods small and resolute. He saw it in their eyes: determination born of shared loss, a bond that held through pain.

As the soldiers slowly drifted away, back to their duties or searching for rest, Falco lingered. He stayed where he was, watching them fade into the dark. They trusted him, leaned on him, and that trust was a weight he knew he could never set down.

Severus stood nearby, like he wanted to say something. But he just gave a small, sharp nod before turning to go.

The torchlight cast long shadows as Falco stood alone. He inhaled, the morning air crisp and cold. They'd completed the mission. They'd brought back the warning. But victory was never a final thing—it was just a pause in the struggle.

Somewhere in the distance, a horn sounded, and Falco's gaze moved to the gates. There were threats still lurking, waiting beyond those walls. But for now, at least, they'd won a fragile, hard-won peace.

The dawn crept closer, light edging in. For a brief moment, he allowed himself to grieve, to feel the ache of the losses. They'd paid a steep price. But it was a price he was willing to pay—again and again—if it meant protecting these men, this loyalty, this Rome.

He squared his shoulders. The burden felt heavier now, and yet it was one he chose to bear. There was no turning back.

Printed in Great Britain
by Amazon